Hidden History

Secret Truth

Green Ef fect Media

Kansas City, MO
www.GreenEffectMedia.com

Green Ef fect Media

The Earth has all the time in the World. And we don't.

—Oren Lyons

The frog does not drink up the pond in which he lives.

—Native American Proverb

Part I

Human ~~Nature~~ *Nurture*

How Far We've Come

*U*nder a blanket of milky white stars draped across a night sky in full regalia, a man looks up in awe and wonders, "Who are we? Why are we here? What is the meaning of life?"

Imagine for the moment that he lives close to nature, separated from the hustle and bustle of the modern world as a few native tribes still do today, but the way humans did for ten thousand generations before the rise of Western Civilization.

I could name a handful of peoples who still live that way. I could name only a handful. There is only a handful left. Their concept of meaning must be vastly different from ours.

Next, imagine that same native visiting one of our ultra modern cities and looking up. "What on Earth happened to all the stars?" he'd ask.

How would you answer him?

◇

For aboriginal tribes throughout history, their destiny, their lives, were inseparable from the stars. The Maya are perhaps the most well-known example. They engineered immeasurably accurate (no pun intended) calendar systems. Their concept of time was not based on human perception of it (like ours is), but intertwined with a the movement of procession stars across the galactic equator.

The stars told time.

Today, our best scientific minds are certain that astrology is a bunch of hogwash. That's likely true. For astrology as we conceive it is nothing more than the Western Mind's limited belief that the heavens control our fate. What truth there is in that is interpreted too simplistically by our world view to remain meaningful.

Our fate is interwoven in the stars. But by no means do the stars control us anymore than we control the lives of honeybees (whose fate is certainly interwoven with ours.)

To the Westerners who cared enough to look up, they looked for auspices that told them what to do, when to wage war, when to do this or do that. Roman Emperors were notorious for this. They were looking for guidance to lead they way. 10,000 years of Western Thought held that humanity is flawed and can't possibly attain any knowledge from looking within. We look everywhere for signs, omens, auspices, leaders, gurus.

Westerners are largely creatures of bad habit.

It makes as much sense as a colony of honeybees looking for patterns in the toxic exhaust billowing from a coal-fired plant to divine where they should build their new hive or how to choose their next Queen.

Yet here we are. Looking for gurus. We find them in cult leaders, religious fanatics and doomsday cults. People have a seemingly intrinsic need to be "shown the path," guided, led. We think ourselves lost otherwise.

That mentality is particular (and peculiar) to our culture.

Astrology is a Western version of mysticism. And it's probably just about as accurate as the Julian Calendar, or inches, feet and Fahrenheit.

Luckily we've corrected a few of our blunders along the way. Yet we still use the Julian Calendar, Fahrenheit and the Imperial system of weights and measures because we Westerners are largely creatures of bad habit.

Aborigines weren't looking for auspices, trying to divine fate from the stars or seeking signs from the Zodiac.

The Maya accurately calculated the Solar Sytem's orbit around the Galaxy when the Western World still thought the Earth was flat. (Ironically, we still do thanks to Economists like Thomas Freedman.)

After a few millennia of blundering, the idea that the stars could tell us when to wage war was eventually dismissed for the hogwash it was. From that "revelation," we made the leap that since stars can't teach us when to wage war, stars really can't teach us much of anything.

We're fatally flawed, know nothing ... but the stars do no better. Despite our faults, we decided we could only rely on ourselves. Owing to our flaws and the stars' ineptitude for prophesying, we determined that we needed to develop technology to guide us through the darkness. So we've enhanced all our flawed abilities with technology. Or should I say, we've enhanced all the flaws of our abilities.

Anything nature can do, humans can do better.

Glasses cover our eyes. Hearing aids plug our ears. TV literally does make the world flat. Bulldozers do the work of 100 men. Cars do the work of 100 horses. Telescopes peer 1 billion times deeper into space than the Maya ever could and tell us a lot more (from which we learn a lot less).

Artificial light replaces the sun ... the Queen of Stars, not only incompetent but so lazy she only lights our sky less than half of the time. What a slouch.

Anything nature can do, humans can do better.

And with the dawn of the electric light, we banished the stars from the sky. Useless points of light. Who needs 'em? Let the scientists keep 'em, the astronomers venture deep into the desert to look at them if they must.

So, how do we answer our Aboriginal man, staring into the lfeless sky above a city when he asks, "What on Earth happened to all the stars?"

I'd tell him:

It was a faulty line of logic that ultimately led to us blot out the stars. It began with an inaccurate belief ('the stars can tell us when to wage war', instead of 'we can learn from the stars') which, when we dismissed, instead of admitting we were wrong all along, we dismissed the stars themselves.

The logic was self-reinforcing. And it progressed across the centuries, down through the generations.

The logical paradigm is flawed and from it precedes a faulty world view. A pyramid with a crack in its base will never stand.

◇

This line of logic about the stars is just one river, one tributary in the Great Flood of Western Thought. It is a metaphor I happen to favor for what's been going wrong all along.

We used to look up at the stars and wonder in awe, "What's the Meaning of Life?" with chill-bumps running down our arms as we considered the unknown possibilities of our existence.

Today, most of the population of the world lives in urban areas where stars are all but invisible. Many of today's urbanites who ever get around to asking "What's the Meaning of Life?" aren't really considering meaning at all, but rather thinking about the meaninglessness of their lives.

Oh, how far we've come.

◇

Our way of life today is on a classic parabolic trajectory towards collapse. If we are to avoid the convergence of the multitude of planetary crises we face, we need first to change our mind-set, our world view, the way we think about things.

There needs to be an evolution of thought.

If You See An Expert
Walking Down The Road....

Recently it seems we've given our lives over to "experts." A doctor is in charge of your health, not you. An investment professional is in charge of your future, not you. Banks are in control of your home, not you.

Not 150 years ago, or even more recently, people were building their own homes with their own two hands. Today construction companies do, while the FDA tells us what we should eat while courts legislate morality.

We need experts to tell us what is safe; we need experts to tell us that something is dangerous. We need the media to tell us what to think.

This is all patently absurd. We ourselves are in control of our own lives, not experts.

Experts. What do they know?

I recall hearing an anecdote once about an impasse NASA was experiencing in the repair of one of its space widgets or another. All of NASA's astronauts and all of NASA's men couldn't put the darned thing back together again.

So they sponsored a contest, challenging grad students in advanced engineering, advanced calculus and quantum physicists to solve their pesky problem.

Realizing this problem was knottier than brain surgery, NASA even asked a brain surgeon or two.

The problem remained unsolved.

This was a veritable Fermat's Theorem (a math problem proposed in 1637 and was regarded as "unsolvable" until it was in 1995.)

NASA passed the challenge on to high schools science fair winners.

The solution remained as elusive as ever.

Until an eighth-grader came along. He didn't supply the mathematics, of course, he didn't answer in specifics. But what he offered was a completely new way of looking at the problem. A way so maddeningly simple.... Well, it made all the NASA folks pretty mad.

But it did solve the problem.

That's the problem with experts. Their thinking is as bound as a bonsai tree.

They are utterly incapable of thinking outside the box.

For a thousand years we believed the sun revolved around the Earth. We toiled for centuries developing complex mathematics to prove it. And we did. We proved mathematically that the sun could revolve around the earth. The math made sense out of our observations of the motion of stars from our perspective on the ground.

The experts had thought the world was one way, toiled endlessly until they found math that supported their belief, and then proclaimed, "We always knew it was true! This proves it!"

But that is the fallacy experts always fall prey to. No "proof" can ever prove that anything is this way or that way. It can only tell us that things can be this way or that way.

Today, we "know" that the Earth revolves around the sun. Because our mathematics tells us so. But another group of mathematical proofs tell us without ambiguity that the Milky Way is indeed a binary star system, two Suns completing an orbit around each other about every 25,000 years.

Our theory that the Earth orbits the Sun may turn out
to be just as inaccurate as the Greek theory,
which had it the other way 'round.

This alternative theory arises from the problems that astronomers observed in the Procession of the Earth. Our planet wobbles like a top as we spin in space. But the mathematics of that procession don't work out precisely unless the Milky Way is a binary star system.

Scientists. Might as well call them Scient-ologists.

This would mean, essentially, that the Earth is merely caught between two stars and only appears to us to be the only thing doing the orbiting. The Maya held this to be true; it's the basis for their calendar's Great Year. If they had used the mathematics we currently use to describe the Earth's procession around the sun (off by something like .0000000001 microns or something) then at the end of the 25,000 year calendar, they would have been temporally displaced by a few decades or so.

Our Julianne calendar, failing to account for procession, makes every fourth year "leap," and every 400 to leap backwards to keep itself pointed in the right chronological direction. Talk about taking two steps forward and one step back. Our calendar has even temporally misplaced the birth of Jesus by more than a week, the pivotal event it starts at.

That's pretty sloppy work, especially for the expert scientific calculation of some fancy-ology or another.

Scientists. Might as well call them Scient-ologists.

For the moment, however, the theory that we inhabit a binary system is not a widely accepted notion.

Our theory that the Earth orbits the Sun may turn out to be just as inaccurate as the Greek theory, which had it the other way 'round.

So why should these guys be telling you to how to live your life? They shouldn't.

So if you see any experts walking down the road, be sure to tell them what they can go do with their precious little theories about the way things should be and ought to be.

The Man Behind the Mirror

I am not an "expert." I hope you don't hold it against me. I have no formal academic training in physics, philosophy, sociology, psychology, anthrolopology or economics. That is a lot of–ologies one can potentially be Expert in, isn't it?

I graduated from a University with a liberal arts degree then picked myself up, brushed myself off and got about the important work of teaching myself how to think.

College is good at a few things, foremost of which may be learning specific skills the human race has developed over the past 8,000 years or so. Unfortunately, one of the most valuable skills we have developed that is not taught at any University I know of, is the ability and desire to think independently.

If I had the wherewithal to found my own university, I believe I would name it The School of Thought. Students could graduate with a degree in Peace of Mind.

But alas, modern academia is a far cry from the idyllic institution of my imagination.

In college, research papers I poured laboriously over, embedded with intellectual fodder, imbued with blood, sweat and tears, never got very high marks. They got lots of marks, usually in red.

In fact, the more didactic the transcription of a professor's lecture, the better grades the papers were given. While these exercises in rote thought seem to demand the undivided attention of many an undergraduate for many an unforgiving hour, I slapped them together at midnight and got As across the board.

This willy-nilly mentality is as much all the rage as excessive alcohol consumption among undergraduates whose mantra is "Cs get degrees."

If I learned anything at all from these exercises in futility, it was that hard work isn't a pre-requisite for graduating college. And thinking even less so.

I am not an "expert." I hope you won't hold it against me.

I learned only, in aggregate, that what college was effectively teaching was no more and no less how to think within a box, whatever that box may be. You are asked to take it on faith where the boundaries of that box are. You are never directly shown the "No thinking beyond this point," signs, though their obscure locations could be triangulated, by those who cared to do so.

But few cared to do so. This triangulation could be achieved (and this is the really hard part) not by attending to what was taught, but by noticing the conspicuous absence of what wasn't.

Through this method of education, to those who do not take notice of the absences, the walls of the box become thoroughly obscured, hidden away right there in plain sight, as invisible as a mirror to a parakeet.

◇

So what makes noticing these absences so challenging? A lifetime lived among small, seemingly inconsequential things to which we have become so accustomed that we can't conceive of life without them. Indeed, we can't conceive of these things at all. They are the mirror, reflecting back onto us a perfectly contained world-view that is indefinitely self-reinforcing, like mirrors in a funhouse. (I hate funhouses. They are no fun, and they make me decidedly claustrophobic).

It was about a decade after college before I could shake off the apathy my education had infected me with. I suppose I'm lucky. Some people surrender to their apathy. I always felt a nagging sensation at the back of my mind, just out of reach, something telling me, no, no, no, you must pay attention to the man behind the mirror.

Think outside the thought process.

My infinite gratitude to some amazing books and authors that were there to help re-reveal to path of learning to me. To illuminate the path. These books brilliantly elucidated the very thoughts that had been nagging at me that I couldn't quite put my finger on.

The books that held a candle to the darkness for me can be found in the Sources and Additional Reading appendix of this volume.

If only in some subtle way, dear reader, do I hope the thoughts on these following pages encourage you to do your own thinking. May they guide you along a path you've been looking for, fumbling for in the darkness.

May my words be always at your back, as you follow your own path.

Down the Rabbit Hole
of Western Thought

The fall of (Western) Man was not from grace, but down a rabbit hole that he thought himself into. He constructed a box and climbed in. There have always been some of us trying to claw our way out. There have been quite a few more who don't see the box at all. Yet the "struggle" to get out is just as unhelpful as being ignorant of its existence.

The truth is, there is no box. Not really, anyway. The only thing we're stuck in is our own minds, our minds which are so conditioned that we can no longer see the forest for the trees, or the world for the box. Our perception of reality is informed by experience as our world conforms itself to the mold of our own design like silly putty in a red rubber egg.

One of the most out-of-the-box thinkers I have ever read, a Transpersonal Psychologist, Joseph Chilton Pierce, claims there is a "crack in the cosmic egg," by which we can escape the box, climb back out of the rabbit hole.

The real rub, though, is this isn't a box or a hole with any boundaries that can be easily experienced by the few senses we recognize.

Our minds have simply been so addled by television, mass media, and the homogenization of shared experience that we are desperately close to a precipice beyond which we will no longer be able to conceive anything that doesn't have a direct physical manifestation within our nearly closed loop paradigm.

That explains why so many of us don't recognize box we're in. It also explains why those who do see it become obsessed with trying to escape it.

Once we become aware of it, their minds seize upon the possibility of a new reality that and think, aha! I see the box! Now

I must plan my escape!

But isn't that a validation of the very worldview we're trying to fight against? The worldview of giving special treatment in your mind to that which you can see.

I'm now aware of this box! I must fight against it!

Why? You weren't fighting against it before you were aware of it. Why start now?

If your head isn't spinning already, you may want to get it examined by an expert. It might be screwed on too tight.

There's another alternative. Now that you see the box, don't expend all your energy clawing at the corners. It will be wasted effort. The box is here to stay.

◇

Historically, every plebeian revolution which seeks to overthrow the aristocracy, it ultimately occurs (after 10, 50, 100 or 500 years) that the plebeians evolve into a new aristocracy. Revolutions don't work because all they do is turn the tables. They never get out of the kitchen.

Civilization has in fact seen so many revolutions that it is by now well-fortified against them. It knows how to defend itself from a plebeian revolt. More, better, bigger guns. And it works. That's not to say that Revolutions aren't won by Revolutionaries and Heroes or lost by Tyrants and Traitors (distinctions made solely by history books).

But it is to say that no revolution has ever been won or lost by either side. The side that emerges victorious simply loses more slowly than their opponent. The fact is, by winning, we are learning to beat the other guy at his own game. But both sides are rolling the same dice, moving around the same board.

And it's deja-vu all over again and again and again. David becomes Goliath.

So what's the solution?

I see the box. The box is made of thoughts and I see the need to change the mindset of the world. What do I do?

Simple. Think outside the thought.

If your head isn't spinning already, you may want to get it examined by an expert. It might be screwed on too tight.

But before we begin the dizzying search for the invisible walls of thought that surround us, penetrate us, bind our civilization together, let's take a step back.

Winds of Change & Blowhards

*D*o *you ya-hoo-oogle?* It sounds like a sound a yodeler would make. But I can't imagine yodeling ever becoming as mainstream as this.

As a society, we are obsessed with finding the one and only truth. Obsessed with knowing pi to a billion decimal places. Obsessed with finding the Unified Field Theory, the ultimate theory of everything, the one truth that binds the universe together.

We are obsessed with statistics. We nit-pick and argue fine-points and semantics.

History, as it's taught in University and high school, is no more nor less than a series of seemingly arbitrary dates. If you know exactly what happened on April 6, 1862, then you truly understand the American Civil War.

Huh? Why?

Meaning is divorced from information, and information wins the War of the Roses.

And when all this meaningless information becomes too overwhelming to process and remember for ourselves, we invent computers to do the memorizing for us. And when those repositories become unwieldy, we invent ways to index the index and the googol bits of information it contains. (One googol is a colossally huge number, 10^{100} — 1 followed by 100 zeros.)

Finding it hard to remember 18 people's 10-digit phone numbers? Here's a hand-held device to do it for you. Congratulations. Now it's guaranteed you'll be incapable of remembering any of them on your own. (Just remember where your hand-held device is.)

While we started out yearning for specifics in order to find meaning, an obsession with accuracy ultimately led us astray from meaning.

If there hasn't been a study done on the harmful effects of breathing in CO_2, (and a study analyzing that first study's efficacy), we're inclined to doubt whether CO_2 actually is harmful. Then a third study comes out and contradicts the first study and suddenly our heads are spinning in circles and we don't know what to believe again. Every time we turn around, the experts are saying something else. O!, we lament, there's so much mis-information out there, how does anyone know what's true anymore?

We lose site of the notion that the biggest piece of mis-information out there is that we have to rely on experts to tell us anything at all.

Native peoples don't understand how we, a people obsessed with knowing everything, have so little knowledge about anything.

We have another, much more powerful tool, one which has sadly atrophied in recent decades.

Common sense.

We need to re-learn how to rely on our own observations of the universe to help us decipher truth from lies from video tape.

Experts who have become the sole purveyors of truth have joined the Industrial Revolution like everyone else. And the product they manufacture and sell to the public: Mass produced thought.

We all think the same way, believe only the things experts condone.

One of my favorite anecdotes comes from David Wolfe's memoirs recounting his experiences living with the native Sng'oi people of Malasia.

This is one of the few remaining hunter-gather groups today, almost completely untouched by the modern world.

Wolfe explains that these people have no written language, but a very strong oral tradition. Their way of life has not changed in millennia, perhaps hundreds of generations.

They do not understand how we, a people they see as being obsessed with knowing everything, have so little knowledge.

We know nothing of the land, the birds, the Earth, we have no connection with the life all around us. We know nothing.

The same has been said of the West by almost every other culture upon First Contact.

The more we think we know, the more ignorant of important things we become.

Our lack of knowledge stems, in part, from the way we think about knowledge. If the Western Mind doesn't possess empirical, scientific knowledge about something, it's not "Capital-T Totaling" True.

In other cultures, understanding is achieved from within, by searching for the soul of something. Meanwhile, the empirical data Western minds look for is external, which blinds us to the truth.

Certainly accurate, specific, precise knowledge is important *sometimes*. For example, GPS systems would be useless if we couldn't calculate seconds down to the 7th decimal place because the bending of time around Earth's gravity would so distort our calculations that the location of objects on the surface observed from space would be off by a mile or so.

But relying solely on empirical data will tell us only where that object us. It won't tell us anything else about that object. And there's so much more to know.

Imagine walking down a urban jungle path. You see a small animal scurry across the path out of the corner of your eye.

"What was that?" you ask.

Your friend answers, "A pigeon."

"Oh, yeah," you say as if now you know what *that was*. You do not. In putting a name to it, you have pigeonholed the poor pigeon, and now your curiosity is assuaged and you're no longer compelled to look further into the question of *what was that?* And so by knowing, you will never know.

The Beginning of Time

*S*ometime in the forgotten past, we starting dreaming of the unknown future and that's when we stopped living in the present.

With the concept of future comes the idea of choice, and that we can make them, and thus, make our own future. With choices, we learn, come consequences. From that concept, we develop a concept of cause and effect.

So, the logic goes, the future can be changed by the choices we make today. Therefore, every future cause has an effect in the past.

And being the questioning beings we are, we decided we needed to know the cause of every effect.

But there were some effects whose causes were unknowable... at least, as far as we knew.

That's when we invented effects to explain unexplainable causes. Mythology, Folklore, Gods.

In this way, the belief in Gods is inexplicably tied to the belief in Future. But what if our idea of past and future exists only in our minds? What if it's no less an arbitrary, imagined concept than say, the Greek God of Time, Chronos, who we invented to explain time itself?

As far as we know, we humans are the only life form on Earth who believes in either Gods or Time.

◇

Animals of all kinds gather at dawn and twilight to watch the sun. Animals certainly recognize its majesty, its beauty, its life-giving radiance ....the miracle of life.

It seem likely that much of life possesses a sense of wonder and awe.

But humans seem to be the only ones to ask, "Why?"

"Why does the sun set? Can I predict when it will set tomorrow? Can I improve on my ability to know that? Can I improve on its ability to set?"

The world is quickly approaching Peak Time and a Global Quickening is happening all around us.

Our compulsive need to know trumps our ability to appreciate, to experience, to just be.

That mentality makes us peculiar. The rituals we perform, the Gods we invent, the ideas we imagine—all in order to explain away the awe of wonder of nature—those make us eccentric.

When's the last time you saw a swan standing in front of a green-screen pointing to some region of the projected map and declaring assuredly, "There's a 30% chance of rain in this area today. And the sun will set at precisely 6:57 p.m."

Ever heard of the *Old-Finch's Almanac*? Does the flock of geese who lined up on the shore of their golden pond to watch the sunset yesterday know it will set today at precisely 6:57?

They probably have an innate knowing of when the sun will set, trusting to instinct instead of relying on a wrist-watch.

For every technology we develop, we lose the ability to do naturally what it now does for us.

Animals certainly realize the sun will set *again* and has set *before*. They know the moon has been full before and will be new again. And they don't need a Julienne Calendar to tell them when.

This innate knowing of *when* and *again* is much different from our concept of future and past.

We think we can tell time. We can't. We can tell what hour of the day it is. We know hours and minutes and seconds.

You can probably tell me how many seconds to microwave mac-n-cheese, but can you tell when you're hungry without looking at a clock and see that its noon?

Wake up in the middle of the night, and you'll ask, "What time is it?" The clock tells you it's 3:30 a.m. What does that mean? In three hours you'll have to wake up and go to work.

I bet you didn't think you were wondering what time will it be in three hours, do you? But you were. You didn't really care what time it was now.

What you really wanted to know is how many hours from now do I have to get up and do something? Is there enough *time* to go back to sleep? As if time is a natural resource we're quickly depleting.

The world is quickly approaching *Peak Time* and a Global Quickening is happening all around us. The price of your time and my time is getting more and more expensive at the pump.

As if time is something we can own.

As if the currency of time is hours and minutes, ticker symbol TIME and traded on the commodities exchange.

Back to our flock of geese.

Our compulsive need to know trumps our ability to appreciate, to experience, to just be.

I doubt they think, "We better finish hunting so we don't miss the sunset! We have a schedule to keep!"

But I bet there right on time, just the same. Because they don't think *in three hours the sun will set.*

When the sun sets, they simply look up, wherever they might be.

In the middle of the afternoon, they don't think about watching the sunset anymore than the sun itself thinks, "I think I'll cast a solar flare at Earth tomorrow."

Most life, I believe, experiences only the present. Birds don't think, "In two months it'll be time to migrate. I hope it doesn't snow before then. I hate the cold!"

Without the concept that there's any way to change the future, the existence of the concept of future is fundamentally different, if not meaningless altogether.

Knowledge of *before* and *again* is not the same as thinking in terms of past and future the way we do.

The past is something to dwell on. The future is something to anticipate or dread. Thinking that the future can be changed is a crucial concept which helps to drive a wedge between past, present and future in human consciousness.

The universe appears and disappears
four-quadrillion times each second.

Without thinking that things can be changed, experience becomes a continuum of connected moments. No *next moment* and no *last moment*. Just this moment.

According to one theory of quantum physics, the universe appears and disappears four-quadrillion times each second.

Within this brief quanta of reality is where conscious perception and experience occur. Each of these four-quadrillionths of a second intervals contains the eternal now. Consciousness, moving from one micro-moment to another, chooses what to carry from one universal moment to the next, creating the illusion of a continuum of past, present, and future. Where only the present exists.

In other words, at this moment I am watching the sun set because at this moment the sun is setting.

At this moment I am migrating because this moment is the moment to migrate.

Past, present and future have no distinction in this way of knowing. The perception of every moment is a present moment.

◇

When did humans lose this ability? What was the great spark that turned our minds into thinking machines?

There's a background din constantly in your head.

There's a sound of swirling thoughts sometimes as soft as the drone of conversation at a restaurant; sometimes as loud as a cheering crowd in a stadium; sometimes it's a song stuck in your head. (I bet you have a song stuck there right now, don't you? And you didn't even realize it until I mentioned it?)

It's always there, that drone. And there's no way to get rid of it. It's like being stuck with a really annoying friend on a road trip. They just won't shut up.

And how many of those background thoughts are about what you're doing right here, right now? How many are about what you're going to do later today or what you did earlier?

We're always wondering, always asking, always anticipating the future, always replaying the past.

It's our grasping minds that creates an arbitrary distinction between past, present and future. And just won't shut up about it.

Sometime in the forgotten past, we starting dreaming of an unknown future. And convinced ourselves we could change it. That's when we stopped living in the present.

So that now, today, and everyday, our brain thinks instead of knows. Grasps instead of experiences. Dreams instead of lives. Wonders instead of awes.

Think Outside the Thought

*W*ake up in a box. From there we get into a box on wheels that transports us to a small box where we sit until we eat a box lunch. They we interact with our illuminated box some more. Now we get back into our box on wheels and return to the box that we own or rent, which itself is composed of a series of smaller boxes. In one of those smaller boxes, we sit for a while and stare into a box that shows us moving images for a couple hours, images mostly having to do with other people's boxes. And think to ourselves that somehow their boxes seem more exciting than ours. When we finally tire of living vicariously in other people's boxes, we stand up and stretch and walk into another box in the big box that we own or rent and lie down on a box spring mattress, where we will fall asleep and dream of one day owning a bigger box.

◇

We are prisoners of our minds, our world view, culture and shared experiences that somewhere along the way have become hardened and crystallized into beliefs we'd die defending. So what does it mean to think outside the thought? I'll begin to answer that question with another.

Out of all the life on Earth, why are humans the only species to look at the natural world with disdain? That thousand-year old

...tree, that's ugly! Build me a skyscraper!. Modern urban jungles are paved, land-scaped, developed scars upon the surface of the Earth, some extending for hundred miles in any direction. They are more easily seen from space that space is seen from the cities. Their light pollution blocks out all but the brightest stars.

Imagine what it would take to be able to see the Milky Way from Downtown Chicago.

To see through the light pollution That's what it is to think outside the thought. . .

It's learning how to see things that were once self-evident, which have become invisible.

Entering Chicago is like stepping into a portal to another galaxy. One where the sky is barren and desolate. A desert. As if it's not in the middle of the Milky Way at all.

It would take a city-wide brown-out to prove the Milky Way is still there, draped overhead, behind the artificial veil.

People live as though in a world apart from nature. It would take a pandemic of world-wide cultural amnesia to prove nature is still here, all around us.

There are truths we have forgotten, destroyed, turned our backs on. But the truths haven't disappeared. Just like the stars, they're merely obscured behind a veil of culture, of modernized life, of technologically-imposed alienation. What are these truths?

Imagine you're born in Chicago, have never been to the country, have never been to the planetarium.

"Mommy, why is

the sky orange?" you ask.

"It's not really orange," she explains. "There's a whole milky way of stars behind it."

All you know is the sky is blue during the day and orange at night. Is it even possible for you to imagine a starry sky?

Without a city-wide brown out, can it ever be possible to see the milky way from Chicago?

Without amnesia, can it ever be possible to Think Outside the Thought?

Cultural Myopia

I can think of a hundred ways I could die before breakfast if I wasn't wearing my glasses. So could the vast majority of people living in the "developed world" who use "corrective lenses."

We don't think of myopia as a pandemic because no one ever dies from it. But worldwide, more people suffer bad eyesight than die from cancer. Hundreds of millions of people rely on corrective lenses absolutely, every second of every day.

Even the Dalai Llama wears glasses. (For someone who reportedly lives on less than $2/day, I often wonder who's his optometrist, and what lab makes his spectacles?)

Optometry is one of the few non-life saving professions that we literally can't live without.

We've built our world around our ability to see, and see well. So how the heck did we ever survive before corrective lenses were invented, a mere few centuries ago?

For the longest time, this paradox plagued me.

In mid 2011, a new invention came along called "HD lenses." No, this is not a new Sunglasses fad straight out of the 80s. These are prescription eyeglasses, which allow you better than 20/20 vision. Superhuman vision.

If these catch on, I have no doubt that people will soon enough be unable to "see" how the heck we got along with "only" 20/20 vision?

"Everything looks so blurry that way," we'll complain. "There's no definition to anything!"

Yet we most certainly are getting along just fine today just as we got along just fine for hundreds of thousands of generations before the invention of eyeglasses.

No technology should ever become *necessary* to live life on

Earth.

Do Eagles who wear glasses to hunt? Does every Eagle ever have 20/20 vision? Are there any microscopic blue-green algae sporting Blue Blockers?

Though perhaps fewer parakeets would attempt flying through glass if only they could see a little better. Hmmm. Glasses for your pet.

No! That goes too far.

We certainly don't need glasses to survive as a species. And neither does your parakeet, dog, cat or hamster.

◇

In 1284, an Italian inventor, Salvino D'Armate, introduced the first wearable eyepieces to the Western World. (Like most things, the Chinese had invented them about 1,500 years earlier.)

But what about all the time in the world before that?

What about fabled Knights in King Arthur's Court or Roman Legionnaires, or Masons or Blacksmiths or, heck, hunter gatherers and farmers? Mayan astronomers? Babylonia warloards? How could the Pharaohs see the tops of their pyramids without glasses? How could a hunter take aim of his spear at a mastodon, or a gatherer find a thorny medicinal herb (well, ok, the thorns might have been dead giveaway—especially if they were poisonous.

The point is, how did human society ever survive long enough to invent glasses if we couldn't possibly see what the heck we were doing? Were we just bumbling in the dark?

Turns out, even asking that question, which seems such a mind-boggling paradox to us today, is a symptom of our own cultural myopia.

In truth, like most other technologies, the invention of the thing itself created a demand for that thing, and a lifestyle developed around that thing until its use became so ubiquitous that we could no longer imagine life without it.

Asking how we got along without glasses is like asking how

we got along without cars. (We didn't live in the Suburbs.)

Glasses have just been around a fair bit longer than, say, an iSomething. But do you think your children's children's children could even imagine a world without their Imaginary iFriend? Likely not, the same way an Suburba-Merican would likely starve without an SUV to drive to the drive through.

A grocery store can be 15-20 miles away from some sub-divisions, across vast, expansive trenches of treacherous highways.

The automobile did not evolve to solve an intrinsic problem suburbanites faced, who were leading unimaginably challenging lives in the absence of SUVs. Suburban life evolved around the existence of the SUV.

And it was the same with glasses.

There were certainly instances where myopic gladiators died in the ring for lack of better eyesight. But this type of problem likely wouldn't have plagued any gladiator for very long. (Gladiators didn't have very long lives, and less so the myopic ones). And legionnaires? Well, someone had to be at the front ranks of the charge. These folks didn't live long either. And your life expectancy probably wasn't significantly impacted by your ability (or inability) to see Hannibal's Elephant-mounted cavalry thundering towards you.

"Don't you see what's coming!?" the one legionnaire cried in a panicked shriek to his blind companion.

"No," his friend stated matter-of-factly, "and judging by the sound of it, I don't envy that you can."

Myopia likely has always effected people as they aged, but likely only the literati (the upper class who could read) were aware of it.

I got my first pair of specs when I was 9 or 10. But until I donned my first pair, I really had no idea what I was missing.

Either my vision had been bad since birth and I had no way of noticing, or it had become progressively worse (and I had no way of noticing).

Gradual changes are harder than you'd imagine to recognize.

◇

Corrective lenses themselves likely have some hand to play in the number of people who need corrective lenses today. Survival of the blindest and all that.

More of us suffer from a "disadvantaged birth" and pass on our dysfunctional genes to our children, who need glasses, who marry myopic spouses, who pass on the gene to their children, and so on. For this reason, today's population is likely visually less acute than our ancestors who lived just 1,000 years ago, before the existence of spectacles.

> Just as Guttenberg's want of spectacles led to the invention of the printing press, it was the invention of the printing press that led to the meteoric rise in sale of spectacles.

Glasses ensure their own existence because each generation who wears them has worse vision than the last. It might even be said that technology is looking out for its own interests, has a kind of survival instinct only seen in living beings.

In his book, "What Technology Wants," Kevin Kelly argues that technology is actually alive, has become so complex that it has developed a kind of "self-organizing complexity." It may even be conscious, possessing enough "knowledge" and "instinct" to actively alter its own environment in order to ensure its own survival.

This is an absurd argument if taken literally. However, the very fact that such an argument could be conceived shows us how we have come to view technology today as intrinsic to our very survival. It offers some fascinating insight into just how dependent our lives have become on technology.

But metaphorically, I think the argument has some merit. Which takes us back to eyeglasses.

◇

People's inability to see clearly at a distance may have had a hand to play in the division of labor.

I'm better at hunting, because I can see that great cat charging from a hundred yards away, so I have a better chance the you of killing dinner than being dinner. But since you can't, you'd better find some other way to make yourselves useful if you want me to share my kill with you.

The onus may have been on myopic individuals (near-sighted) to creatively devise something they could do with their lives in the absence of long-range eyesight.

This could have been a driving force in the creation of fine art (requiring a meticulous attention to fine, precise detail that can only be appreciated close-up.)

More economically practical professions may have arisen from myopia, as well. Such as blacksmiths, masons and other professions requiring close-up attention. Presbyopia (far-sightnedess) is much less common than myopia (near-sightedness), but tends to afflict people more as they age.

◇

Fast-forward several thousand millenia.

As every technology begets a life suited for it, with the invention of glasses, a crucial event in human history occurred.

Guttenberg did as much for optometrists as he ever did for printing. As many bibles as he sold, he would have died a wealthy man selling glasses to read them.

Anecdotal evidence suggest that Guttenberg himself was near-sighted, possibly contributing to his interest in the meticulous, close-up demands of the creation and implementation of moveable type.

Had Guttenberg been fitted with a pair of spectacles in his youth, he may never have taken an interest in the tedious, mind-numbing profession of moving little jigsaw letters around all day.

Just as Guttenberg's want of spectacles led to the invention of the printing press, it was the invention of the printing press that led to the meteoric rise in sale of spectacles.

A few hundred years later, the invention of the automobile necessitated even more sales of eye-pieces—as much for drivers to negotiate a high-speed world as for unwitting passers-by to dodge them.

Technologies like 250mph race cars, tiny iWhatever screens, newsprint, and many others would never have been invented or used without the pre-existence of corrective lenses.

While a wide range of diverse disciplines and professions may never have existed at all if everyone had perfect vision, the technology of today exists only because now we all do have perfect vision.

Today, corrective lenses have become so pervasive in our society that even as they have "corrected" our eyesight, they have made our cultural worldview myopic.

We can't see how the heck we possibly got along without them.

The Hundred Years' Culture

*T*here are hundreds of examples of technology infiltrating our daily lives. It goes without saying we can live without all of them. It goes a little further to say we'd be better off without most of them. There are even a few pieces of tech that I'd argue make our lives miserable.

But regardless of your opinion of individual technologies, the key point is that almost none of them existed before the Industrial Revolution. And most are younger still.

The world you live in, the world you think you know, is less than 100 years old.

There are very few harbingers left of the Old Way of Life. And very few of the things we do today could have been done at all a century ago, let alone conceived of.

There have been more fundamental changes in your lifetime than in the past 1,000 years. The world you know is not the world your grandmother knew. Not even remotely.

This has never been the case before in all of human history.

Every opinion you have ever developed of the world, anyway you have every thought about anything, indeed any thought that ever popped into your mind is a product of the past 100 years.

No one in the history of the human race has every thought the same way you do, right now, with your brain wave patterns affected by technology and a rapidly always-evolving culture.

Ancient ways of life, daily rhythms, ways of doing things, traditions, that had endured for thousands of years, changing very little from one generation to the next, are now being wiped away perhaps several times in a single generation.

Cultural consciousness, generational memory, experiences handed down over thousands of years used to serve as cultural bridges and span across untold numbers of generations.

Today, cultural consciousness, generational memory, is surrendering its "free will" to choose what to carry from one generation to the next.

Today, Windows 3.0 is ancient, DOS a relic of a by-gone era.

Can you even remember a world without computers? A world without telephones? A world without electricity? A world without automation?

The rise of technology has been meteoric.

The world is changing at an ever-accelerating rate.

The universe may appear and disappear every four-quadrillionths of a second, but is there no limit to how many generations of iPhones can exist in the same amount of time?

People Will Believe Anything

(Even that they will believe anything)

It's a common axiom that People are Stupid. We will believe anything.

We believe believing anything is a symptom of our stupidity. Is it true? When, where and how did the idea that people are stupid develop?

The belief is everywhere. Pervasive. Go to a beach on the lake or ocean and surely you will see the sign, *No lifeguard on duty. Swim at your own risk.*

Well, why should there be?

For hundreds of thousands of years people have been swimming in the lakes and oceans without lifeguards. Now suddenly, we need lifeguards to help save us from drowning?

Well, kind of. The need for a lifeguard is untwined with the idea of private property. The beach is owned by someone, and if someone else drowns there and there is no sign, look out for a lawsuit.

Yes, lifeguards save lives, no question about it. But that doesn't answer the underlying question of why we believe that people need experts to protect them? That without our protectors, a Sunday swim will turn into a feeding-frenzy for lawyers.

There are thousands of Caves in the United States alone. All converted to tourist attractions, raking in the dough. There are signs, here, too. *Slippery when wet.* Gee, ya think? Do I really need a sign to tell me that?

The belief people need to be told these common sense things is a real slippery slope. Is common sense really not so common anymore?

◇

On February 27, 1992, Stella Liebeck, a 79-year-old woman

from Albuquerque, New Mexico, ordered a 49-cent cup of coffee from the drive-through window of a local McDonald's restaurant. Liebeck was in the passenger's seat of her Ford Probe, and her grandson Chris parked the car so that Liebeck could add cream and sugar to her coffee. Liebeck placed the coffee cup between her knees and pulled the far side of the lid toward her to remove it. In the process, she spilled the entire cup of coffee on her lap. Liebeck was wearing cotton sweatpants; they absorbed the coffee and held it against her skin, scalding her thighs, buttocks, and groin. Liebeck was taken to the hospital, where it was determined that she had suffered third-degree burns on six percent of her skin and lesser burns over sixteen percent. She remained in the hospital for eight days while she underwent skin grafting.[1]

The legal justification for the suit was that McDonald's "gross negligence" for selling coffee that was "unreasonably dangerous" and "defectively manufactured."

A judge ruled in favor of Liebeck for $640,000. The Media panned the case as the poster child of frivolous lawsuits.

Was it?

> The belief actually isn't *people are stupid*.
> It's *other people* are stupid. People who believe
> people are stupid never think of themselves that way.

One was to look at this is the Obi-Wan Kenobi-ism, "Who's the more foolish? The fool or the fool who follows?"

Liebeck's medical expenses were in excess of $18,000 (a lot of money in the 1990s). The same medical treatment today, just 20 years later, would have been well over 10x that amount, considering in most cases a minimum of $10,000/day for a hospital bed. Not to mention legal fees.

Yet Leibeck wasn't suing for $600,000. She only asked for $20,000.

In a society engineered to believe people are stupid, we have set up elaborate methodologies to protect people from their own stupidity (lawyers) and allow Corporations to defend themselves against their customers' stupidity (lawyers). The legal framework of a lawsuit is merely a symptom of a society founded on the notion (among others) that People are Stupid.

Coupled with the notion (not shared by any other "developed" country in the world) that people have to pay for their own health care, that it is not a necessity bound to the Commons, suddenly it doesn't seem as far-fetched to sue McDonalds for hot coffee.

Yes, Leibeck's stupidity was her own. But how could anything else be expected of her?

McDonald's ultimately didn't make their coffee any less hot, but just put an idiot-proof warning on the cups in two languages, "Coffee is extremely hot." I'm not sure what good that's going to do for public safety if you really think people are stupid (are they really going to read it?)

But in the absurd logic we've created, a *disclaimer* is enough to prevent McDonald's for being sued again.

◇

You gotta make everything idiot proof, *because there's always an idiot.*

Can't you just see that huge sign hanging overhead, flapping in the breeze? It's hanging right over Kansas, I would imagine, right in the middle of our country so everyone can see it. No offense to Kansas—there's nothing particularly wrong with Kansans, except perhaps for the occasional one managing to get sucked up by a twister (Could Dorothy have sued The Wicked Witch?)

It's almost a religious belief as ingrained as the notion that people are born with original sin.

The belief actually isn't *people are stupid*. It's *other people* are stupid. People who believe people are stupid never think of themselves that way.

So if we all believe it about others, but not about ourselves, is it just our own stupidity that we don't realize how stupid we are?

Seems to me the myth of the stupid person is several-fold.

1)We always need someone to blame something on. We'd rather die than admit we are wrong. People may not be stupid, but we certainly are stubborn.

2) Stupidity is profitable. If we believe people are stupid and, realizing that, some of them are stupid enough not to make everything idiot-proof to allow for other people's stupidity, then if some idiot didn't make whatever it is idiot-proof, then the other idiot who got burned, injured, whiplashed, slipped on wet concrete, or otherwise suffered distress, has the God-given right to sue the first idiot who didn't make the thing idiot-proof in the first place.

This self-reinforcing logic works only if we believe people are stupid.

Lucky for us, this notion is continuously re-enforced everyday.

Every public place has signs warning us about everything from hot coffee to wet cement to *you break it you bought it* (evidently threatening people makes them not do so many stupid things) and of course "piso mojado" on bathroom floors. At least stupidity doesn't discriminate.

In addition to signs in public buildings, television is the number one reinforcement of this notion. Inside the little box, we learn about people's absurd mis-adventures in 20 minute sit-coms.

If the belief that people are stupid isn't just a culturally reinforced myth, and there really are real stupid people in real life, they most definitely can be found on television.

[1]Wikipedia.
http://en.wikipedia.org/wiki/Liebeck_v._McDonald's_Restaurants

Believe This, Not That

*T*he *world is* round, according to Eratosthenes. Who? The World is Flat, according to Thomas Freidman. Oh, I know who he is. An economist.

So which is it? Round or Flat? And who is Eratosthenes?

Friend to no economist, Eratosthenes was a curator of the Great Library in Alexandria before it was sacked and burned by the Christians, whose religion was slowly rising to ascendency over their previous "cult" status. Ever since, the Knowledge of the modern world has seemingly depended less on truth and more on convenience.

For Columbus, it was useful for the world to be round. For outsourcing jobs, flat is a better deal.

If you were a two-dimensional being, the world would be indisputably flat. If you are a three-dimensional being, the world is indisputably round. Unless you're Tom Freedman.

But don't worry, this isn't a political rant.

What if you were a five or six dimensional being? Would the world be hyperspherical?

Does our opinion of the world's nature change the nature of the world? I believe it does. Our world-view shapes our world-to-view.

The practicality and profitability of an idea very much biases our minds and put words in our mouths about the feasible or laughable nature of an idea.

The acceptance or rejection of an idea has a tremendous power to change our lives and our world. But the ideas we accept or reject often have little to do with their efficacy, and more to do with how useful their practical application proves to be. Sad to think that the world may not have electricity at all if J.P. Morgan Chase hadn't believed Edison's idea could make him some money. And by that I mean to express, of course, my fear and loathing of the Banks.

For Columbus, it was useful for the world to be round. For outsourcing jobs, flat is a better deal.

Would Einstein be remembered today had E=MC² not been seared into the public's mind by its offspring, the atom bomb?

Or consider Alfred Nobel, who created the Nobel Prize so that dynamite would not be his only legacy. Yet Nobel would have no legacy at all had there first been no dynamite. Space travel, too, may never have materialized without a Cold War to win, Communists to race to the moon.

History is replete with any numbers of scientific ideas which have been relegated to the realm of "pseudoscience." They've never made it past that stage of "laughable," or "patently absurd."

Imagine how irreconcilably different the world would be if some things had never been accepted.

Imagine how irreconcilably different the world would be if other things had.

Yet in many cases, there is as much demonstrability of these concepts as any other. I've put together a short list. As you read through, you will find yourself laughing out loud, and proclaiming, that's a ridiculous idea! Complete hogwash!

But keep an open mind. Who stands to make money if this alternate idea is accepted? Who stands to loose?

I hope you find yourself scratching your head on at least one or two of these, wondering, could that really be true? Could that actually be the case?

For me, I find the line between science fiction and science fact to be a bit blurred around the edges.

Let's start with some easy ones.

Ready, here goes. Fact or fiction?

• Ultra-efficient automobile engines can get up to 100 miles per gallon on diesel. These engines cost up to 50% less manufacture.

• Every home in the world can produce enough solar energy to exceed its needs. Solar panels can be purchased and installed for about the cost of 1 household's annual energy costs.

• 100% organic farming techniques can feed a family of 4 for $30 a week, and can support up to 10 billion humans.

So, true or false? Believe it or not, the list above is already happening in various countries in Europe.

Would Einstein be remembered today had E=MC2 not been seared into the public's mind by its offspring, the atom bomb?

There's no obvious reason these models can not be copied the world over. Except, of course, if we're feeding ourselves and producing all our own energy, well, where would all the Capitalists go? Wouldn't Peter, Paul and Mary like to know?

The further down the list we get the stranger things become. Here's a few ideas that are pretty hard to believe.

But remember to keep an open mind. Which of these are really hogwash and which do we only think are hogwash? Can you find any that we currently accept as truth that may not be?

• The contemporary of Edison, Nicholas Tesla, developed a theory of electricity that trumps Edison's. Tesla's energy is limitless and "free" and is derived not from man-made power but rather exploits the invisible electric current naturally occurring in Earth's atmosphere.

• The Sun creates its energy not from internal nuclear reactions (a theory that suits our "nuclear age") but rather from external sources – the invisible electric and gamma rays naturally occurring in deep space.

• The Pyramids were power plants from Ancient Atlantis that implemented the same theory that Tesla "discovered" 10,000 years later.

• Almost forgot, the pyramids and Sphinx are 10,000 years old, not 3,000. Proof? Erosion of the Sphinx matches that found in a tropical rainforest (like South America where the other Pyramids are). The Sahara desert was a tropical climate in 10,000 BC.

• Our civilization is 30,000 years old, not 10,000. A major worldwide catastrophe (probably the Great Flood) annihilated Atlantis in 9,500 BCE. Civilization managed to rebuild, but forgot about Atlantis and thought the Egyptians built the pyramids without knowledge of the wheel or even a single pulley.

Any sufficiently advanced technology is indistinguishable from magic.

Let's keep going. As I promised, the further down the list we go, the stranger and stranger things become. And here is where it gets harder to distinguish fact from fiction....

• We're being watched by alien UFOs (Unidentified Flying Objects) controlled by an alien race.

• We're being watched by satellites controlled by NASA and Fox News. These satellites orbit our planet and can both view stars in the Andromeda galaxy and the time on your wristwatch. They can also pinpoint the location of an object on the ground accurately within a nanometer while it's moving faster than the speed of sound.

• All of the knowledge of the Universe is contained within an invisible library of knowledge encoded in light rays that we can access with the hidden power of the pineal gland in our brains. Collectively, this depository of knowledge is called the Akashik Records. No one knows who built it. Some claim the Atlanteans. All the information contained within can be encoded in crystals or embedded in light waves.

• All of the knowledge of the Universe is contained within an invisible library of knowledge encoded in binary code that we can access with invisible wifi signals. Collectively, this depository of knowledge is called the Internet. No one knows who built it. Some claim Al Gore. All the information contained within can be encoded in binary code or imbedded in microchips.

◇

Sometimes the things we accept seem more preposterous than those we reject. British Author Arthur C. Clark put forth these three laws:

1. When a distinguished but elderly scientist states that something is possible, he is almost certainly right; when he states that something is impossible, he is probably wrong.

2. The only way of discovering the limits of the possible is to venture a little way past them into the impossible.

3. Any sufficiently advanced technology is indistinguishable from magic.

Perhaps it's not so important to decide what is science fact and what is science fiction. Perhaps it is more important to understand that the laws regulating what our culture believes to be science fact and what we dismiss as science fiction are neither arbitrary nor do they conform to any cosmological constant.

(And of course we all know that we don't know what the cosmological constant is, only that there must be one because our understanding of the universe doesn't make any sense without it.)

The laws we have formulated for distinguishing fact from fiction are just as incredible as the fiction we accept and often more incredible than the facts we dismiss.

It may prove more useful to understand why we believe what we believe than to understand exactly what it is we believe. Because often, what we believe doesn't make any sense.

Through a Looking Glass, Darkly

For a hundred thousand generations, humans gazed into the starry skies and asked, "Where does the sun go at night? Why do points of light glow in the sky? Where does the wind come from? Where do we go when we die?"

Aside from that last one, in the past five generations, we've convinced ourselves that we've answered just about every question we've contemplated over the past three million years.

Now if you have a question, all you need do is ask Google and the answer lies waiting for you. Just click *I'm Feeling Lucky.*

But we haven't answered every question.

We've just stopped asking new ones.

The fundamental building blocks of the universe we can see is not something we can see at all.

Oh, sure, we have particle physicists asking, "Where the heck is that darned Higgs boson?" and things of that ilk.

And of course *you're* asking, what the heck is a Higgs boson?

A Higgs boson is a theoretical subatomic particle that endows every form of matter with mass. It's also known as The God Particle. (We'll get to that in a minute.)

You see, protons and neutrons and electrons are virtually mass-less, so even the billion trillion quadrillion of them in the souls of your shoes don't add up to a hill of beans. In other words, a billion of nothing is still nothing. If all you were made up of is atoms, you wouldn't be made up of anything at all.

Realizing this, physics postulate the existence of the Higgs boson, a particle a billion times smaller than the nucleus of an atom, yet having a billion times more mass. It's this "invisible weight" that makes a bowling ball 40lbs and a pencil 5 oz and a human 200 lbs or so. (Significantly larger humans are the result of too many steroids or Big Macs).

Point is, without the hypothesis of the Higgs boson, out current understanding of the model of the universe we cling to with such unyielding tenacity doesn't work.

And if it didn't, we'd be in big trouble. All the answers to all the questions we've been asking for the past hundred thousand generations would be called into ... question ... again.

Where does the sun go at night? Why is it bright? Where does the wind come from?

All those answers hinge on our fundamental "reductionist" and "materialist" understanding of the universe. In a word, we believe the building blocks of the universe can be reduced (hence reductionist) to matter (hence materialist). Without matter, the universe wouldn't exist. (Sounds obvious to you, doesn't it?)

Yes, of course, so why did I even see fit to mention it? Of course, the universe is made up of matter.

Or is it?

Is the sun really hot because of nuclear reactions of various particles of matter?

> Like dark matter, dark energy and the tachyon, the Higgs boson was "tacked on" to an existing theory to make it work with everything we think we know.

You probably never heard of them, but there have been equally plausible (and mathematically proven) hypotheses in the past. (All have been abandoned since Einstein, who showed us how an atomic view of the universe is useful.) But it's not the only theory. Seeing the sun as atomic simply fits well into our outlook in this age of atomic power. Nichola Tesla proposed the sun was inherently electrical. (Making it fundamentally a ball of energy, not matter). Yes, even though Einstein told us that matter and energy are interchangeable. In our world view, energy is subservient to matter. But is it? Did the chicken really come before the egg?

Whether the universe is primarily energetic or materialist makes a rather large difference.

Until a few short human life spans ago, the smallest component of matter as far as we knew was an atom. The Greeks gave us that.

But around the time of Einstein, Atoms didn't really work anymore as the smallest irreducible particle, so we "reduced" matter further and found protons and neutrons and electrons. Well, that solved a few problems, but these things really didn't have any mass, so why do we?

The universe detectable by light waves and eyeballs is only a small fraction of the entire universe "out there."

Gotta be that we simply haven't reduced things far enough to understand them yet. Let's go deeper!

Aha, there it is! I see it! It's the Higgs boson. A billion times smaller than an electron, with a billion times more mass.

The only trouble is, no one has actually seen it. It's theoretical. Like dark matter, dark energy and the tachyon, the Higgs boson was "tacked on" to an existing theory to make it work with everything we think we know.

Turns out that while we believe matter is the building block of the universe, that theory only works if a theoretical invisible particle serves as the building block for matter. Makes perfect sense, doesn't it? How many of those can fit into the souls of your shoes?

An alternative physicist and proponent of the Biocentrism theory, Amit Gosswami, says that it makes no sense at all.

Looking for the invisible Higgs boson is just as ridiculous as Catholic Monks who whittled away the Middle Ages arguing how many angels could sit on the head of a pin.

The fundamental building blocks of the universe are not something we can see at all, Gosswami says. Because, you see, the universe detectable by light waves and eyeballs is only a small fraction of the entire universe "out there." It belies our human-centric world view that we believe the universe visible to us is all there is. And since we have to invent things we can't see anyway in order to make everything we can see consistent with the theory that that's all there is, we need to stop looking for things we can't see and admit the universe is based on something else entirely.

Wow, my head's spinning.

We only ask questions we think we know the answers to. And then devise experiments to find the evidence we're looking for.

Let's reduce what I'm trying to say to simplest terms. We might have been forced to accept that the Earth isn't at the center of the solar system or that the solar system isn't at the center of the universe, but we still act as though we believe humanity is at the center of creation. We are fundamentally beings of matter (not mind or spirit or ether ... we think), and therefore, so too, is the universe made fundamentally of matter.

This is so pervasive a concept that the underlying ideology leading to that belief has been obscured by a hundred years of "accepted" theories being formulated along the same rigid lines, which become self-reinforcing.

Better said, we only ask questions we think we know the answers to. And then devise experiments to find the evidence we're looking for.

If you devise an experiment that's engineered to find certain results, it's likely to produce the results you expect. And if it doesn't, we usually claim the experiment was flawed, and set about devising a new experiment (not developing a new theory).

A billion billion dollars has been spend building the Large Hadron Collider which is supposed to find the Higgs boson. Do you think we're likely to give up until we find it? Oh no, we'll find it one way or another .... Even if we have to invent it along the way.

◇

In fact, we've answered none of the questions that have haunted us for a hundred thousand generations: Why do points of light in the sky glow? Where does the wind come from? Where do we go when we die?

Let me say that again.

Instead of finding answers to our fundamental questions, we've merely found the answers we've been looking for.

The fundamental building block of the universe may not be matter, nor energy, not chickens nor eggs, but consciousness.

Those are answers that are consistent with the logic of our illogical worldview. All our answers take as their unquestioned premise that the universe is made of matter and so are we. Our model of the universe hinges on that. If we believe in our model, we have answers to all our questions.

But there are other models.

For example, the mathematics for the Earth revolving around the sun works just as well as the mathematics for the sun revolving around the Earth. (It's just a much, much, much, much longer equation—but it works.)

So what if we suggest a new model?

According to Biocentrism, the fundamental building block of the universe is not matter, nor energy, not chickens nor eggs, but consciousness.

Not ours. But the consciousness of the universe.

That theory offers resolution to some very fundamental paradoxes: namely, the nature of energy and matter; science and God.

And what of the Higgs boson?

Well, as Pierre-Simon Laplace once said of God: "I have no need of that hypothesis."

Ironically, as monks in the Middle Ages were contemplating how many invisible angles could sit on the head of a pin, nature-based aboriginal tribes and Obi Wan Kenobi arrived at the same notion that "alternative" physics is arriving at today: That consciousness—spirit—is the Force that surrounds us, penetrates us, binds the universe together.

Nature-based religions have taught this from time immemorial. We are one with the world. Not separate. Not apart. One. Same as the mountains, the birds, the wolves, the trees, Mother Earth.

They teach that each of us, by direct observation, can know the answers to all our questions. We can have an intimate relationship with the universe around us. All we have to do is tune in and pay attention.

The closest 6,000 years of Western thought ever brought us was, *turn on, tune in, drop out*. Failing that, we've decided that the fundamental "truths" out there are inherently unknowable. But we've set our best minds to the task!

The commoners, the rabble, they certainly can never grasp these things! If there's any hope at all, we need to have an intellectual elite to answer all these questions for us! The way the world operates is too mysterious for us to ever understand by direct observations! By God, we need priests and monks to understand the mind of God!

Nature-based religions and Obi Wan Kenobi arrived at the same notion that "alternative" physics is arriving at today: Consciousness—spirit—is the Force that surrounds us, penetrates us, binds the universe together.

Though we may have turned our backs on priests and monks during the "enlightenment," we still didn't turn away from the fundamental ideology they had always propounded: that we needed someone, someone *smart*, an intellectual giant to explain the world, the universe, the mind of God to us.

Today's monks today have traded in their brown-hooded cowls for white lab coats, but their job description hasn't changed much in over six thousand years of Western Thought. (Though they are getting paid considerably better today.)

Tell me, Father, how many angels sit on the head of a pin?

Tell me, Doctor, how do we find the elusive Higgs boson?

Appropriate, isn't it, that we call the Higgs boson the "God particle?"

By God, we need priests and monks to
understand the mind of God!

Physicists' quest for the Holy Grail is taking them ever deeper into the obscure quantum reality of a probability field surrounding a theoretical Higgs boson particle.

As the questions become more and more complex, designed to root out ever more elusive answers, our "intellectual elite" become more and more removed from direct observation.

I thought the whole point of reductionist physics was to reduce to universe to ever-simpler elements. Why is it then, that the more we reduce, do we keep getting more complicated answers?

Does this question-answer duality truly reveal the fundamental reality of a mysterious and incomprehensible universe? To me it seems more plausible that the exponentially increasing complexity of our methodical interrogation of the Universe belies only our own pathological eccentricities which continue to lead us ever more astray--deeper down a rabbit hole of an endlessly convoluted, incomprehensible and ever-more irreconcilable world view.

None are more hopelessly enslaved than those who
falsely believe they are free.

—Goethe

Part II

What you don't know *you don't know* ^
~~can't~~ hurt you *can!*

*(Absurdities so absurd you just
might not find them hard to believe)*

Pineal Envy

According to the World Health Organization's (WHO's?) International classification of diseases department, there are an estimated 10^{30} illnesses (physical and mental in aggregate) that can infect any given human at any given time. Of course, 10^{25} of the pathogens have yet to be categorized. But you might have one of them anyway, even if you don't know it and your doctor can't diagnose it.

One that we *have* diagnosed is the Highly Sensitive Person syndrome. HSP for short. Turns out, as good as Western Medicine is at categorizing, it's proven even better at acronym-izing.

About 10% of people "suffer" from an extreme sensitively to loud noises, bright light, large crowds, a general feeling of being overwhelmed and a chronic case of claustrophobic in both small spaces and large cities.

> Perhaps the conscious signature of nature is not so subtle after all but is merely drowned out by our artificial world of abhorrent sounds, lights and constant speed.

In other words, their "heightened" senses serve to make them feel somewhat out of sync with most modern, "civilized" over-stimulating environments.

Large cities. Traffic. Ambulances. Driving at night. Bright, artificial light. (The sun isn't a problem, so the notion that they're sensitive to all light (like albinos) is debunked.)

It's the extreme contrast between light in the dark (which primarily comes only from artificial light) that causes them almost debilitating discomfort. Myself, I find it almost unbearable to drive on a dark Interstate highway at night with a car approaching from behind (especially ones with those new, should-be-illegal

LED headlights.)

The Highly Sensitive People people describe their environment with all its over-stimulation as stark, loud, devoid of sentience, naked, sterile and empty; they feel that the constant flood of over-stimulation prevents them from "experiencing" the world. In contrast, patches of Earth in which they're able to sense nature is what they mean by a vibrant world filled with substance, and teaming with consciousness.

Modern science, in its quest for knowledge through learning has il-legitimized all innate inner experiences of the world.

Such places are oftentimes today only found on preserves, National Parks, or other areas specifically legislated to be protected. Without that protection, make way for the bulldozers.

Being able to sense nature requires what many modern people would consider a fine tuning of the senses. But perhaps the conscious signature of nature is not so subtle after all, but is merely drowned out by our artificial world of abhorrent sounds, lights and constant speed.

And this is what it's like to be in the world of a Highly Sensitive Person. But the truth is, we all live in that world; most of us have just managed to numb our senses as a coping mechanism.

.I believe the experience of being human just 100-200 short years ago (before the age of Science and Industry) was a fundamentally different experience—one teaming with sensations and experiences of the natural world few of us today will ever know.

Shades of this HSP "disorder" affect me, though not as severly as others I've spoken to. I do need to shut out loud sounds, large crowds, inner city suffocation and bright lights.

I believe there is another way to look at this experience.

Instead of viewing this as a disease, I believe the highly sensitive people people, the 10% of us, are the few remaining folks in the West who's senses have not become comfortably numbed to artificial life.

The highly sensitive people people find peace and tranquility in nature to a higher degree (a higher sense) than most folks. They're usually quite good at meditating. They can stop their minds from running away with their thoughts—a concept other folks even have a hard time "wrapping their mind around." What does it even mean to "stop your mind." Does that mean stop thinking?

Science is obsessed with answering every question it contrives by applying the scientific method to the problem, whose holy mantra is, "nothing unprovable is true."

No, it means to start experiencing.

The existence of the highly sensitive people people shows us just how calloused and shut off from our world we've made ourselves.

◇

David Wolfe, a psychologist who has lived immersed in various modern anthropomorphic societies (the few that remain), describes a seventh sense of "knowing." This transcends a sense of the mystical, which might be the sixth. A sense of knowing means a sense of feeling the earth and the other beings who are part of it. It also includes having an inexplicable sense of knowledge of the world—"knowing" without learning.

Natives know where medicinal plants grow, they feel a kinship with other life, an inter-connectedness. And that echoes the very thing that highly sensitive people feel is so utterly lacking, in the modern world.

It could very well be that all non-Western people living out of the "civilized" world are what we would term highly sensitive. If so, their experience of heightened sensitivity would be anything but the overwhelming experience we attribute to the syndrome. Their experience would be a sense of inter connectedness, wonder and awe in a world teaming with life and spirit all around them. This would be a world they'd feel as attuned-to and connected with as sufferers of "HSP" feel closed off and alienated from.

Modern science, in its quest for knowledge through the teach-er-pupil relationship, has il-legitimized all innate inner experi-ences of the world. It is obsessed with answering every question it contrives by applying the scientific method to the problem, whose holy mantra is, "nothing unprovable is true."

These Western scientists have recently pinpointed a specific physiological difference between native peoples all over the world and modern Westerners.

That difference is the size of their pineal gland.

Theirs is significantly larger than ours.

The pineal gland is a region deep in the brain, just above the spinal chord.

Western medicine has identified little practical purpose for the pineal gland. Yes, sadly, in Western folks, that's probably the case.

Not only is the pineal gland smaller in the Western Hemisphere compared to other humans, but it's smaller compared to most other life forms on Earth. Western studies frequently report that the pineal gland "in humans" is 1cm wide. But that's definitely not the case in many aborigine peoples.

Eastern esoteric traditions have always associated this gland with psychic abilities. Yet western textbooks regard it merely as a calcified vestige of the third eye. A third-eye, science says, is merely a organ we've lost in the process of evolution, and is just your standard, run-of-the-mill, well-developed light-sensitive organ. It goes without saying that a third eye has nothing at all to do with the soul according to the Scientific method (which, it goes without saying, has nothing at all to do with the soul.)

Western medicine admits the pineal gland affects sleeping patterns and the circadian rhythm—our body's "internal clock," which is a phenomenon we can't explain. It's as if our minds have an intuitive sense of the rhythms of the Earth, the moon and even the stars—an ability which, according to Western medicine, shouldn't be possible.

Other than making the impossible possible, Western medicine has identified little practical purpose for the pineal gland. Yes, sadly, in Western folks, that's probably the case. It serves little useful purpose. Especially no "practical" purpose in terms of helping us cope, survive, thrive in the modern world.

To suggest the pineal gland might have a function, that it might be associated with a heightened state of awareness, contradicts everything Western medicine doesn't know.

But Western medicine admits there's a link between the subconscious and the pineal gland, vis-a-vis, REM sleep.

Native aborigines such as the Jivaro (a Native American tribe) and the Sing'oi people of Malaysia have a concept of reality quite dissimilar to ours. They regard the dream world, an altered form of consciousness, as the real world. The best way we can understand their concept of the dream world is to relate it to what we understand as the spirit world—though that's a very one-dimensional notion of a very vibrant universe beyond our "physical world" shadow world, which aborigines consider a mere illusion. In many ways, it is, Western theoretical physicists would agree. Some of them have described the world we hear, touch, taste, smell, and see as a kind of projection of the true nature of reality. Imagine a film projected in a movie theater. If somehow, the characters on the screen really were alive, they would still have no sense that they were a projection on a screen, being watched by other people in the "real world."

Further, just as a film projection is no more than a series of stills projected in very fast succession, our universe actually disappears and re-appears four quadrillion times ever second. (Don't ask me to explain how or why. I can't. But some theoretical physicists will tell you there's math to prove it).

Aborigines would no doubt tell you they don't need to prove

it. They spend much of their time (even their waking hours) in what we might consider a trance-like state of spiritual consciousness which is barely tethered to this physical world, which is very impermanent. While in this trance-like state, they talk of experiencing the true nature of our intimate connection to living Earth around them, and a heightened sense of awareness of the natural world—the true nature of the world.

Also, while in this state, Western studies have shown heightened activity in the pineal region of their brains.

◇

To suggest the pineal gland might actually have a function, that it might be associated with heightened state of awareness, contradicts everything Western medicine doesn't know. I have looked in vain for studies done on the pineal gland and highly sensitive people people. I am not a scientist myself, and have no desire to be imprisoned by that mindset. So don't go suggesting I should do a study like that myself.

> If it's true that aborigines have something civilized people lack, that's a secret Science would rather take to its grave than admit.

If I were a cynical person, I'd say those studies haven't been done for a reason; or they have and the results haven't see the light of day.

If a link is shown to exist between sufferers of HSP and their pineal gland, it would overturn an idea that's crucial for keeping the West in its trance. It would mean there are adverse consequences to the modern society we have developed; that we've actually lost innate abilities in our mad rush to technologize the world. And that is something we will never admit.

It would also mean admitting that aborigines have something civilized people lack, and that's a secret Science would rather take to the grave than admit.

With all their stubbornness, sham and drudgery, it is obvious that Westerners aren't thinking with their pineal gland. Except perhaps the 10% of highly sensitive people people, whose pineal gland is actually functioning.

<>

Of further interest:

Ayahuasca, a medical plant found in the Amazon, has a rich legacy of spiritual traditions, myths, therapies, rituals and aesthetics, spanning from the primordial roots of the indigenous tribes of South America.

It has been prescribed in the West as a "cure" for the HSP syndrome, suggesting a definite connection of some sort between spiritual "powers" and HSP.

Modern Medicine's Chronic Disease

Modern medicine has become extremely good at what it does best. The only problem is what it does best is not curing disease.

Where it truly excels is finding new diseases. Medicine doesn't actually create its own diseases in a laboratory; the diseases do that themselves. Nor is the pharmaceutical industry some kind of mass production facility for new biological weapons.

Although you wonder sometimes when people actually get sicker when they're admitted to the hospital. You see, hospitals are like the spa where diseases of all varieties come to relax, unwind and do some networking after a hard day's work.

> Modern medicine has become extremely good at what it does—turning us all into hypochondriacs.

Modern medicine has an uncanny knack for catching new diseases, almost on a daily basis, it seems. Kind of makes you wonder if the AMA has the locker rooms in those spas bugged. (No pun intended)

Whenever modern medicine catches a new disease, the pesky little problem of what the heck to do with it arises. And what it loves to do more than anything else is categorize new diseases into nice, neat packages and deliver them to the pharmaceutical companies tied up with a pretty bow.

Yes, modern medicine has become extremely good at what it does—turning us all into hypochondriacs by categorically categorizing every little pejorative pain, annoying ill, chronic cancer discreet and discomfort we have. 10^{30} is a 1 with 30 zeroes after it. That's how many diseases we've categorized since the beginning of modern medicine a mere century ago (that's a 1 with 2 zeroes after it.) Talk about productivity!

I think categorizing all of these diagnoses is counter-productive. It takes away the common sense element of figuring out for myself why I'm sneezing. And makes all of us, every day of our lives, believe we must take something.

People today are sick. One in three Americans has a symptom that chronically manifests.

It makes common sense to assume that many of today's known diseases didn't exist before the Pollution Revolution.

Our environment is polluted. Living in Chicago, an x-ray of a human's lungs reveals small black spots, now considered to be normal living under the polluted air.

◇

Chemically analyzing our tap water reveals traces of every pharmaceutical known to man. Corporations dump hazardous chemicals indiscriminately into rivers and streams and seas. People pour drugs expired or unused down the kitchen sink. And so on.

And all the while, probably 10^{29} out of 10^{30} of the diseases we've categorized didn't even exist 100 years ago.

It also makes common sense to assume that many of those diseases simply didn't exist before the Pollution Revolution.

Common sense tells me that all the diseases known to man today are not diseases at all, but merely symptoms of the same disease. Every human body reacts differently, but the same disease is the one caused by our toxic environment.

Ironically, despite the hoard of diseases we've categorized, the one making all of us sick is one we don't recognize.

By curing so-called disease, modern medicine is only making patients more comfortable by numbing their symptoms.

There is no curing being done at all. And there can never be until we understand the nature of what's infecting us all. It's all

caused by 1 of 2 things, either toxicity (our polluted environment) or deficiency.

Even our organic vegetables have only trace amounts of the
vitamins and minerals they contained 100 years ago. Mostly,
that's due to our eroded soil.

Ironically, despite the hoard of diseases we've categorized, the
one making all of us sick is one we don't recognize.

Some studies that have been debunked by the AMA (Which
for my money is a strong endorsement *for* their efficacy) suggests that mega-dosing on vitamins will cure almost anything,
including cancer.

What!? Vitamins and nothing else will cure every disease
known to man?

No, there's really one 1 disease. And, yes, vitamins can cure it.

Ok, wait, how can vitamins cure cancer.

They don't. Cancer is a symptom caused by a deficiency of
vitamins. Restoring balance in the body eliminates the symptom.

And everything "illness" is a symptom. And, together, our
symptoms are trying to tell us something. It's time we listen
instead if mega-dosing on pharmaceuticals, which, in studies
debunked by the AMA, actually make us sicker.

This is Not a Bright Idea

*I*ncandescent light bulbs are illegal! At least, they will be by 2014. It's a provision of the Energy   Bill signed into law in 2007, which asserts that incandescent bulbs use too much energy, and mandates a complete switch over to fluorescent lights.

Personally, I'll be switching to candlelight after my stockpile of mercury-free bulbs is depleted.

Little known fact: fluorescent bulbs contain mercury. And the   FDA issued this warning (paraphrasing):   If a fluorescent bulb is dropped and shatters, open all windows and doors and ensure your home is well-ventilated for at least five hours. Then, take the shattered fluorescent bulb, place it in a well-sealed plastic bag or Tupperware container and place it in the trash.

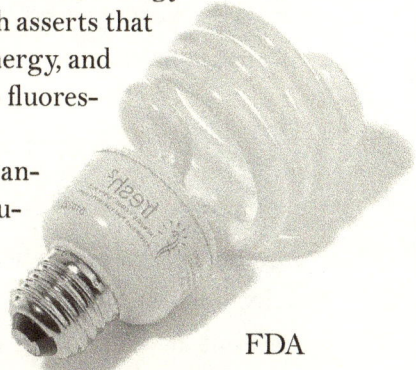

Great. Then what? If you're lucky enough to avoid mercury poisoning from the bulb itself, the carcass will end up in a landfill, where the mercury is likely to leach into the ground and, ultimately, the water table.

So what's the point of this move away from incandescent bulbs? Oh, yeah, incandescent bulbs use too much energy, which is bad for the environment.

You know what they say about Edison's tried and true light bulb, which has been in continuous use since 1880. It's the worst light bulb ever invented, except for all the others.

But by all means, let's try switching to mercury bulbs. Despite the criticism, I just have a gut feeling it'll work. Who signed this 2007 Energy Bill anyway? Oh yeah, George "go with your gut" Shrub. Chalk one up for the Republicans' valiant efforts to save the environment. I thought they didn't even believe in global warming?

In 2005, Senator Inhofe (R-Okla) said, "Global warming is the greatest hoax ever perpetrated on the American people" ... next to all that nonsense about mercury.

The entire issue is patently absurd. Literally.
This level of absurdity could be patented.

I get it now. So how much energy will the switch save? Supposedly, if every American citizen changes just 1 light bulb to fluorescent, it will save the equivalent energy of 800,000 "full-size" automobiles over a 1-year period.

So, let's see ... US population 310 million, one bulb apiece ... get my calculator and ... oh got it. According to these statistics, the energy consumed by 387 incandescent light bulbs is equivalent to the energy usage of just 1 "full-size" automobile. Excellent. We're on the fast-track to fix the environment now!

I have a better idea. Heck, tugging on Superman's cape, spitting into the wind and pulling the mask off the ol' Lone Ranger are all better ideas. But how about this. What if every suburban SOB and soccer mom trade in their SUV for a hybrid?

Remember the "slug bug" thing? I don't get that. What is it about watching a VW drive by that incites red-blooded Americans to violence? Why do these ruffians begin indiscriminately throwing punches at whoever happens to be standing next to them when they see a beetle drive past? I don't know. But I'm certain these are the same people behind the wheels of the monster Chevy 4x4s prowling the suburban highways. And this time it's going to be my little Honda hybrid that gets squashed like a slug bug as the Monster Trucks careen down suburban straight-aways that been transformed into 24/7 SUV rallies, drivers in-cited to violence whenever they see my vulnerable little Honda.

I'm all for going green, but if "they" legally enforce the use of fluorescent bulbs, the infamous "they" are all mad as hatters.

Exactly what is it that people are hauling aside from 60-gal-lons of gasoline in their tankers anyway? Are they transporting Joshua tree trunks? Or just their obese offspring to McDonalds?

"Full-size" automobile? More like "super-sized."

Which leads us back to light bulbs.

Switching to fluorescent bulbs for the energy savings seems like someone ordering an extra-value meal breakfast burrito and asking for artificial sweeter in their coffee because sugar causes obesity.

So, assuming the average distance between McDonalds loca-tions throughout the 48 contiguous United States is 2.5 miles, and the average SUV boasts all of 18 miles per gallon (hybrids can get 50; EU standards call for 100!), and McDonalds serves 52 million people every day, how many gallons of gasoline are used driving to and from McDonalds on a daily basis? Include in your answer that the average drive-through wait time while your gas-guzzlers idles is less than 3 minutes.

Advanced algebra? I think not. Allow me to rephrase:

How many McDonalds customers does it take to screw in a fluorescent light bulb?

The entire issue is patently absurd. Literally. This paints absurdity in a whole new light (pun intended). This level of absurdity could be patented.

How many McDonalds customers does it take
to screw in a fluorescent light bulb?

Then again, every little bit helps! Devouring your 800-calorie breakfast burrito? That's fine as long as you save those 15 calories from the sugar in your coffee. Driving your 4x4 or SUV to McDonalds? No problem as long as you're willing to use mercury-filled halogen bulbs at home.

I'm all for going green, but if "they" legally enforce the use of fluorescent bulbs, the infamous "they" are all mad as hatters.

Incidentally, the phrase "mad as a hatter" arose in the 1800s when hatters manufactured top-hats out of animal hides treated with mercury. Exposure to mercury caused the hatters to literally go mad. Imagine what wearing all that mercury on their heads for so many years did to people … and their offspring.

Speaking of Republicans, where are the big-government naysayers when you really need them!? They who fight tooth and nail for firearms are nary to be found when the government wants to outlaw incandescent bulbs.

Makes you wonder if the whole thing is a scheme cooked up by the lobbyists for the Mercury Miners Guild of America. From my understanding, it wasn't long after the lid could no longer be kept on the mad hatters mercury (no pun intended) that the time-honored practice of modern Dentistry put down roots (pun intended).

And now that the ban has been lifted on publicly speaking out against the use of mercury amalgam, the halogen bulb begins to shine brighter than ever.

Hold on, you're not actually laughing out loud at these horrible puns, are you? It's gotta be the mercury then. It's already affecting your brain.

The whole world is going mad. Mad as a hatter.

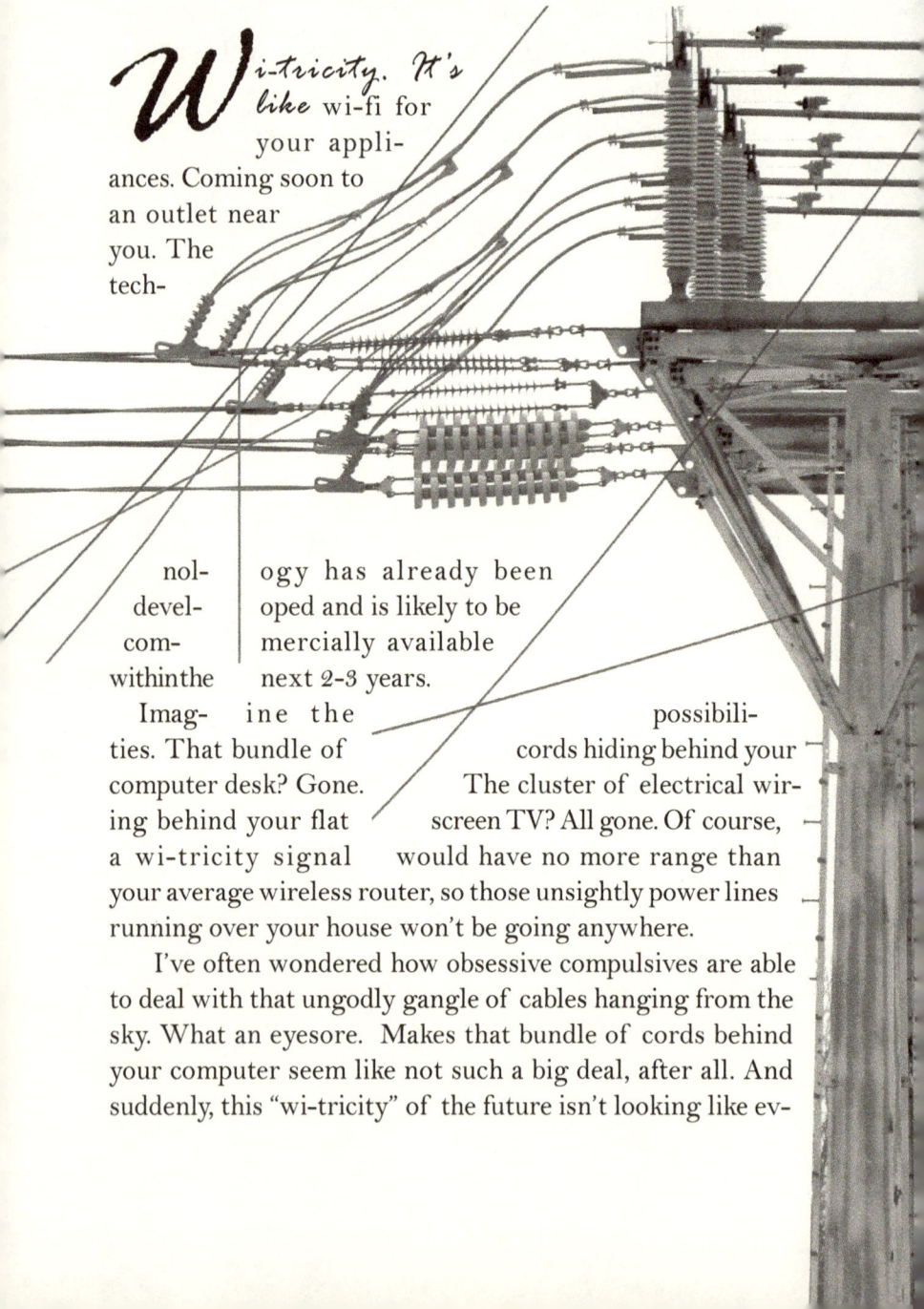

Wi-tricity? Why not?

*W*i-tricity. *It's like* wi-fi for your appliances. Coming soon to an outlet near you. The tech-nol-devel-com-withinthe ogy has already been oped and is likely to be mercially available next 2-3 years.

Imag-ine the possibili-ties. That bundle of cords hiding behind your computer desk? Gone. The cluster of electrical wir-ing behind your flat screen TV? All gone. Of course, a wi-tricity signal would have no more range than your average wireless router, so those unsightly power lines running over your house won't be going anywhere.

I've often wondered how obsessive compulsives are able to deal with that ungodly gangle of cables hanging from the sky. What an eyesore. Makes that bundle of cords behind your computer seem like not such a big deal, after all. And suddenly, this "wi-tricity" of the future isn't looking like everything it's cracked up to be. True wireless electricity would do away with that unsightly mess in the sky, too.

Sound like science fiction to you?

Actually, it sounds exactly like what Nikola Tesla—Thomas Edison's one-time assistant, life-long arch-nemesis and proverbial mad scientist—accomplished in 1899 when he illuminated 200 light bulbs from a power source 26 miles away.

Nicola Tesla pioneered the world's first "alternative energy" a century before there was anything we needed to find an alternative to.

Nikola Tesla—the Moriarty to Thomas Edison's Holmes—offered the world a fundamentally different way of understanding the laws governing electromagnetism, an eloquent theory that outshone Edison's comparatively crass, unwieldy, model.

Imagine living at the end of the 19th century. The world-view held at the time was that electricity was a mystical force with chaotic and unpredictable properties. Tesla lent credence to that belief with his infamous Tesla Coil, which, during one public demonstration, reigned down a violent, crackling lightning storm onto an unsuspecting and terrified crowd gathered to witness this new form of wizardry.

Tesla became the very epitome of a mad scientist, lightning bolts arching from his fingertips. In the public's eye, his kind of electricity represented the Dark Side of the (electromagnetic) Force.

◇

The grid was born in the burgeoning industrial age. Edison helped de-mystify electricity in ways the 19th century public (and his investors) could grasp and accept. He demonstrated that electricity could be harnessed and controlled through the advanced machinery of the great Industrial Age.

Edison's light bulb was an idea ripe for the picking. It easily won over a superstitious culture groomed to believe that only civilization's newest, largest, loudest machines would allow mankind to conquer the world and tame nature's fury. And it was very compatible with capitalism. Money could be made by making electricity.

Thus, the "modern" day electrical grid was born, which, a century and a half later, has grown to mythical proportions, sprawling haphazardly across the globe.

Electricity was the proposal that transformed the wide open West and East and everywhere in between into a knotted clusterfudge of cables marring every landscape both urban and rural.

Obsessive Compulsive Disorder isn't a pre-requisite for being appalled by this ghastly vision of technology. In June 2010, National Geographic referred to the The Grid as an "awkward, inelegant contraption ... a kludge in desperate need of overhaul and repair."

That sprawling metallic Atlas, upon whose shoulders the entire infrastructure of the world now rests, is nothing more nor less than a loose confederation of independent power plants conscripted to the endless marathon of generating the ever-increasing amount of power required to run the modern world.

The Grid is frequently brought to its knees by central air conditioning during the hot summer months, heaving with black outs and brown outs in its futile quest to match energy consumption with production. And it must match—precisely—every hour of every day. If an energy surplus is generated, the excess voltage overloads the grid. Alternately, a draw that outpaces production places undue strain on relay stations that then desperately attempt to re-route preset pathways in order to deliver additional power to areas of heaviest consumption. There is no infrastructure in place to save up energy for a rainy day—no battery or battery back up for The Grid. Demand must constantly, precisely keep pace with supply. Day and night. Forever. Something about this is reminiscent of watching a dog chase its tale.

Ever since the technology behind it was initially bankrolled by J.P. Morgan Chase, humanity has been obsessively building an electric world for itself. The past century's colossal undertaking to construct The Grid speaks more to its viability for generating a profit than the practicality of generating electricity. Yet as you can clearly see if you're reading these words on your glowing computer monitor or simply sitting indoors at night, the technology of The Grid does stagger along, albeit oftentimes with a limp and always ineloquently.

In June 2010, National Geographic referred to the electrical grid as an "awkward, inelegant contraption... a kludge in desperate need of overhaul and repair."

Sadly, an idea itself is only secondary when considering its potential to change the course of human events. The nebulous line between a good idea and a bad idea is transcended by ideas which are useful, profitable. Given that definition, The Grid is an enormously useful construct, a sound business model supported by the Classical theory of economics that makes the world go round. Consumers of electricity represent the ultimate captive audience, and the Masters of the Grid the ultimate monopoly.

Which sounds more like science fiction to you? A futuristic landscape pockmarked with power plants and substations, low voltage and high voltage and extra high voltage towers, an immeasurably vast, sprawling gulag, a crisscrossing kluge of crackling wires shadowing the infrastructure of a chaotic world? ... Or, Tesla's worldview of an ordered universe, eloquent in its simplicity—a universe in which it is not Classical Economics that makes the world go round, but rather a tangible force called electromagnetism that could be harnessed directly from Mother Earth?

Perhaps the better question is, in which world would you rather live?

Tesla's Free Energy

*T*he *billions of* dollars and man hours that went into developing the infrastructure of The Grid—not to mention maintaining it for the past century—has been completely, unimaginably, unnecessary.

There may never have been any need to generate electricity at all. Nor any need to conduct it through the kludge.

Electricity is already here. Already everywhere. And just a tiny pinch of it can power anything.

Tesla offered the world wireless electricity—wi-tricity as they're calling it these days, which we now know is possible to achieve even within the framework of The Grid.

But Tesla one-ups Edison even here. Unlike a wireless electricity router The Grid would have to employ, there is theoretically no terrestrial limit to the range of Tesla's wi-tricity. That's because his kind of power isn't generated or dependent on a man-made grid at all.

If Earth generates a magnetic field, it must also generate an electrical field, meaning the world is one colossal power plant, a lending library of free electricity.

Energy harnessed from water falling over a dam can be used to generate electricity. Tesla proposed the same principle applies to the rotation of the Earth, which is constantly falling through space. (Bear with me; I know this sounds crazy.)

Space is not a vacuum. So, as our tiny blue sphere hurdles through space, rotating, energy is released and an electromagnetic field is formed. Tesla theorized that in addition to Earth's magnetic field (evidenced by the North Pole and the South Pole) Earth also has invisible electrical field.

Out of modern day quantum mechanics, one theory in particular has arisen which lends credence to Tesla's notion. Physicists since Einstein (whose work Tesla's preceded) view electricity and magnetism as two sides of one unified force, known collectively as electromagnetism. So if Earth generates a magnetic field, it must also generate an electrical field, meaning the world is one colossal power plant, a lending library of free electricity.

Further, Tesla claimed to have determined Earth's resonance frequency, thereby demonstrating how energy from its electrical field could be harnessed and transmitted anywhere on the planet. Literally. Wirelessly.

If any of this is true, the implications truly are mindboggling. There would be no need to choose between clean coal and natural gas. No need for big oil companies at all. No oil spills and no global warming. No nuclear power plants. None of that would exist because there would be no need for energy production. Tesla's theory provides all the energy the world can possibly consume and then some—at virtually no monetary cost, and certainly no ecologi-

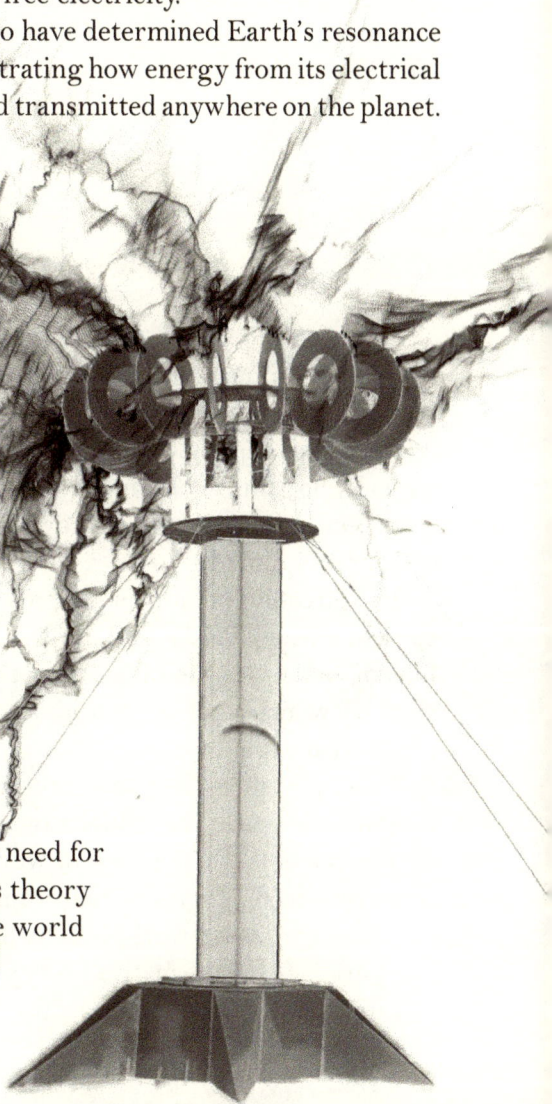

cal price to pay. Our needs are exceeded a thousand times again by a freely available power source right beneath our feet. No drilling, shalling or fracking required.

In theory, every home ever constructed could simply have a Tesla Coil installed in the basement, and the energy needs of the household would be met. For free. Forever. Had history been written in Tesla's favor, the entire concept and need for "alternative energy" today would be irrelevant. Of course this theory of "free" energy nursed from Mother Earth herself is, to this day, unanimously dismissed by mainstream capitalists, and scoffed at by the scientific community.

In the public's eye, Tesla's kind of electricity represented the Dark Side of the (electromagnetic) Force.

So let's not lose sight of reality. In the materialistic world we've built for ourselves, Tesla remains the very epitome of the proverbial "mad scientist." The few rogue researchers who have continued his experiments into the modern day have done so with virtually no grants nor funding, and their very promising results have been summarily ignored by their peers. Not rejected. Not disproven. Ignored.

The direction of human progress seems to parallel the road to riches, whose road signs, in turn, we read through the foggy lens of our worldview. Shouldn't the possible give rise to our worldview instead of our worldview governing our convictions about what's impossible?

There have been frequent forks along the path of progress. Imagine the world that could have been had we taken just one of the roads less travelled—a world forged from beneficial, non-profit technologies arising from a mindset of cooperation, not competition—a world in which Nikola Tesla's concept of the world's first "alternative energy" was implemented a whole century before there ever was anything we needed to find an alternative to.

String Theory

(and Brass and Woodwinds)

L *et's take* a foray deep into science fiction, just to have some fun. First, we grant that Tesla's theory of spinning Earth wi-tricity absolutely beyond reproach. Free electricity for all. Enough to power cars, planes, space ships, even time travel.

Further, let's also give Tesla's power to Ancient Atlanteans. They generated such power on a massive scale with the "Power Plant at Giza," a.k.a. the Great Pyramid. Here's your last stop before the real fun begins on our ride into sci-fi.

Just like oil fields running dry, if we ever suckled enough "Tesla power" from the Earth, stole enough of its fuel, surely its orbit would simply decay and we would careen into the sun.

So, the Atlanteans knew how to harness the amplitude modulation of the Earth into electricity. So what happened to that great civilization? Where did they go? And why has their ancient technology been lost to us?

Atlanteans realized that the energy of the Earth could not possibly be limitless. Just like oil fields running dry, if we suckled enough "Tesla power" from the Earth, stole enough of its fuel, surely its orbit would simply decay and we would careen into the sun.

Could we ever use that much energy?

In 1890, when the first geyser of black gold gushed forth, do you think Jeb ever thought that someday the world would possibly ever be running out of oil? Inconceivable!

Or not. The Atlanteans approached the threshold at which Earth could give them no more. And still it was not enough.

Next in humanity's perpetual quest for bigger and better things, our greatest civilization discovered the amplitude modulation of the sun.

Travel throughout the Milky Way became possible using the power of Stars.

But stars, too, have their limit. Suck to much of their energy and they collapse into black holes.

Let's survey the carnage so far. Destroyed Earth. Check. Destroyed the sun. Check. Destroyed the solar system in the death throws of our star. Check.

Now we're onto the vibrational resonance of our galaxy. Which we harness for interstellar travel. Now we're into Andromeda.

But even that's not enough.

As far as theoretical physics go, anything that can happen, does happen, in some alternate reality.

Now we discover the vibrational resonance of all the strings in string theory. And not just the strings. But the woodwinds and brass, too. The entire orchestra of the universe, playing for humanity!

And we build massive universal-scale Tesla coils capable of sucking the very energy out of the universe itself! Out of the very continuum of space-time!

We use that energy to manifest man-made black holes capable of warping space time.

Theoretical physicists have actually postulated that artificial black holes could be created, if only we had access to an endless energy reserve. And now we've found just such a reserve. The vibrational resonance of strings.

As far as theoretical physics go, anything that can happen, does happen, in some alternate reality. And since nothing is impossible, just highly improbable, and I've imagined this scenario, it follows it must have happened already.

And in that end-game, after humanity destroys the universe and all the galaxies in it and all the stars in them, we send the final human child born in the last moment before the final ember of the final star flickers out back through the worm hole which we created that destroyed the universe.

We send that child back to ancient Earth where it all began. At all costs, by any means necessary, he must destroy Atlantis before they perfect their technology and happens all over again.

The Sedona Effect

I was born on a warm day at 11:06 AM, just in time for lunch, my mother said…. No, wait. Sorry. No need to start back that far. (Although it's true.)

About 10 months ago (that's better) something in the deep recesses of my brain "clicked." Maybe some forgetful Yogi left a door into the Akashic Library unlatched and it blew open in the wind. But that isn't likely since the entire premise of a forgetful Yogi seems absurd.

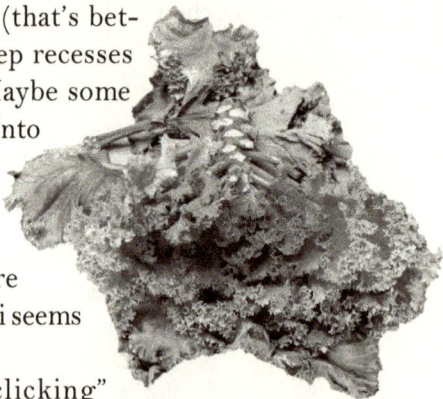

When I heard the "clicking" sound in my ear, the first thing I did was look over my shoulder to be sure it wasn't some member of the San Tribe a.k.a !Kung People (phonetically: click-Kung) sneaking up on me from behind. Nope, no one there.

I realized then it wasn't a click at all and hadn't manifested in my mind, but was in fact my stomach growling (this is a common mistake made among carnivores).

"I need a salad!" I exclaimed.

A salad? What? Did I say that out loud? I was not a salad eater!

In college, I'd always made a bee-line for the meat, prompting one of my friends to comment, "Man, I have just one question for you … do you eat enough meat?" as he eyed my plate of greasy, high-fructose corn syrup laden, GMO-fed, hormone infused, towering pile of BBQ ribs.

"No," I said proudly, carnivorously consuming the carrion

and then buzzing back to the buffet for my second serving. (Or 10th, depending how you define a serving.)

But please don't think I'm a horrible person! Despite my penchant for ravenous ravinity, I still recycled, have never held a Corporate Job, didn't vote Republican or own stock in Martha Stewart's company. I wear size small carbon shoes and never step in wet cement. (Making a carbon footprint.)

By diet I do not mean a weight-loss regimen, but rather its other, lesser-used meaning: what one chooses, through conscious decision making and planning, to put in one's mouth.

The Incident With The Meat was about 10 years ago. I'd hit rock bottom, and I'd since backed off such Senatorial-Roman-Style gluttony, but had never, ever, ever in my life uttered the words, "Man, I just don't eat enough Kale!"

Yet suddenly, here I was, 2010, and feeling a desperate craving for a salad. Maybe it was the vibrational resonance of the people around me. Maybe I was just waking up. Maybe it was the vortexes.

Vortexes?

Yes, my metamorphoses started in Sedona. On vacation in that New Age oasis in the Arizona desert, I consumed a salad that did not consist solely of iceberg lettuce, croutons, bacon and green eggs and ham for the first time in my life.

◇

What initially put Sedona on the map was the discovery of its now-famous vortexes by far-out-there New Age pioneer Page Bryant in the 1950s. She claimed she was channeling the spirit of an ancient Native American Chief who had intimate knowledge of the Earth. Bryant claimed the vortexes were Earth's chakras.

And in the 60s, when the New Age movement really gathered some steam, people from all over flocked to Sedona and took a page from Paige's book and themselves got sucked into the mythology of vortexes.

Sedona has since become so fringe and lost in the mists of the New Age, that the energy there is now powerful enough to corrupt even the most carnivorous carnivore into craving salad!

So, in Sedona, consumed by the power of the vortices, I meandered into a healthy-whole-food (not a grocery) store and purchased some purple-stemmed produce I later learned was called Kale, which I eyed at the time with all the wonder of a child.

By cooking, we change our food, and by eating it, change ourselves.

"What is this remarkable, oddly-shaped thing! It's not perfectly round, has no waxy coating and it's probably not the least bit sweet or salty! And I've never seen anything this fluorescent that wasn't a Pokémon! Surely this thing cannot stem from the same tree of life as I! Perhaps it has stepped out of the Shadow Biosphere, but more likely it's from another planet entirely."

(I'm exaggerating because it amuses me to do so.)

Nevertheless.

Since then, I cannot believe the changes I've made. After we returned from Sedona, I learned Kale was indeed of this Earth, chanced upon a very interesting book (a bit on the fringe for a novice, but that's ok) called "The Sun Food Diet Success System," and visited the Borrowed Earth Café, a local raw food restaurant.

I loved the title of the book almost as much I loved the not-cheese lasagna and not-cheese, not-chocolate cheesecake I devoured at the café.

Notice that there are a lot of nots in this brave new world. Not-cheese, not-grocery store, not-chocolate. Someone should not-hire a not-marketing agent to come up with some not not-terminology for all these things!

In any case, my habits of not-diet, for which I affectingly

adopted the term "SunFood Diet" (see, how hard was that?) took a quantum leap immediately. And by diet I do not mean a weight-loss regimen, but rather its other, lesser-used meaning: what food one chooses to put in one's mouth through conscious decision making and planning.

My metamorphoses started in Sedona where I consumed salad that did not consist solely of iceberg lettuce, croutons, bacon and green eggs & ham for the first time in my life.

For these past 10 months I have slowly been transitioning completely into Raw Food Diet-ism, which is now for me about 90% vegetarian, of which perhaps half of that is raw foods.

But the most important thing -- the vortex around which my whole SunFood Diet revolves -- is avoiding processed foods. Certainly no fast food or high fructose corn syrup. Ever. Oh, and you must absolutely do a peanut-butter-banana-chocolate smoothie every morning! (Better than Atkins shakes; good for – ahem-- digestion.)

But there are other everyday foods that we all know collec-tively know are "bad for us" but we all say, "oh I don't care." I'll offer a few examples.

•Soda - I replaced with water & lemon or tea).

•Artificial Sweetener - I replaced with agave or organic honey (the jury for me is still out on Splenda)

•Pasteurized dairy products - I replaced with flakseed for eggs, almond milk, and I have a wonderful recipe for herb ricotta cheese that involves nothing but cashews, filtered water and dill!

•White bread- I replaced with whole grain bread.

•Russet (white) Potatoes. Monocultures are as bad for the soil as white starch is for your teeth (as it gets processed by the body it turns quickly into fat.). So since two wrongs do not a good potato make, I replaced Russets with Sweet Potatoes or Squash.

•Soy! (very, very processed and hybridized.) This should be called Soylent Green (think the Charleton Heston sci-fi classic from the 1970s.)

•Activia! (Not that I ever used this processed product in the first place. I merely needed to manifest another moment to tout the all-important importance of the peanut-butter-banana-chocolate smoothie every morning.)

Now, please don't take the above list as my way of taking out the laundry on every form of nourishment known to man or hanging you out to dry for eating of the forbidden food.

All of the above are simply shown to illustrate foods which we eat today that are man-made hybridizations or processed varieties of natural nutrients. And I believe that if you look for examples of these, and slowly wean them out of your diet, you will notice a dramatic change.

Not long after the vortexes in Sedona were "discovered" by Paige Bryant, and hippies hopped to Sedona en masse, Bryant left, saying, "The people here are too weird!"

I lost 40 pounds in the first year of the Sunfood diet, and weight loss was not the intent. I never considered myself fat at 180 pounds, but that was actually considered obese for being 5" 7'. And, what's more, the "normal" weight for a human on standard BMI charts has slowly been creeping up over the years. The new "normal" is now as much as 10 lbs higher than ever before.

The concept of "raw food" is founded partially on the notion that the act of cooking itself is a form of "hybridization and alteration" to a food's natural form. By cooking, we change our food, and by eating it, change ourselves.

So, for example, steamed cabbage is as different from raw cabbage as, I don't know, a cheese pizza is from a cow.

Just food for thought. Literally.

But take all this with a grain of salt.

Remember Paige Bryant who discovered the vortexes in the first place? Not long after the hippies hopped to Sedona en masse, Bryant picked up and left, exclaiming, "The people there are too weird!"

Yet if she never discovered the vortexes in the first place, those new age souls would never have flocked to Sedona where they became infected with "the weirdness."

And if she had never discovered the vortexes, not a single vacation would ever have been taken, or retirement home built, or Chevy commercial or John Wayne movie filmed there. No one would ever have heard of the sleepy little town in the middle of the desert. And at least one carnivore would never have found salvation.

I guess that's what you'd call the not-butterfly effect.

The Tiny Blue Spot

cyclonic storm of epic proportions assaults the planet's northern hemisphere, burying everything in its wake. At its largest measurable point, the storm consumes nearly 10% of the surface area of the entire planet.

Hard to imagine? Not really. The Great Red Spot on Jupiter can be seen right from your backyard with an amateur astronomy telescope.

It's not your everyday storm. Scientists tell us the "Eye of Jupiter" has been around for the equivalent 400 Earth years. What they mean to say is that for a long as they've had telescopes powerful enough to see it, the Spot has always been there. In one of the solar system's greatest ironies, the Great Red Spot formed on exactly the same day humans invented the telescope!

That sounds pretty amazing, doesn't it?

But there's something even more amazing. In the last days of January 2011, a storm raged on Earth that rivaled the size of Jupiter's Great Red Spot, which is roughly 25,000 miles across. Jupiter itself is approximately 280,000 miles in circumference.

In comparison, the Earth's equatorial circumference is roughly 24,900 miles, and the Great Blizzard of 2011 spanned 2,500 miles.

The ratios of storm size to planet are eerily similar.

On Earth, the Great Blizard of 2011 produced "thundersnow," an extremely rare meteorological event when thunder and lightning accompany snow. The conditions for both are rarely

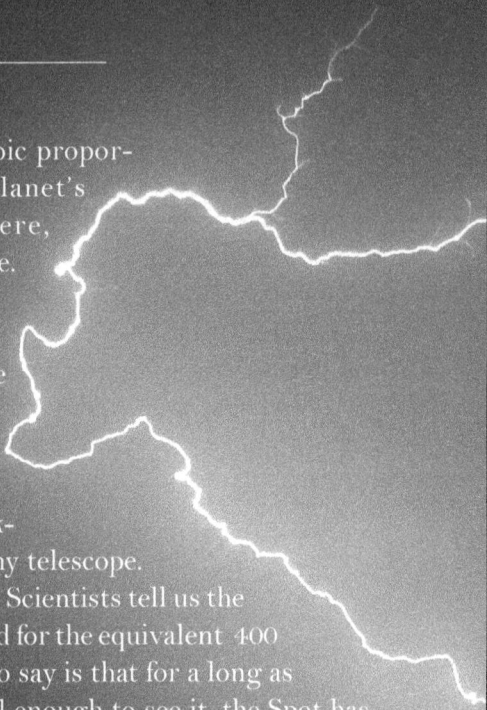

more severe and cataclysmic every season. It's the same story across the globe: hundred year floods hitting every year. Record snowfalls, droughts, hurricanes and all manner of severe weather are assaulting civilization on a global scale.

◇

Really? Is the weather really that bad? Heaven knows the news media is notoriously prone to sensationalizing everything.

Rage, Revolution and Ratings in the Middle East!, headlines proclaim. Not to dismiss the gravity of events occurring in the region, but that's a rather melodramatic headline, even for the mainstream media.

But the ever more severe patterns emerging in meteorological events from the rare (like thundersnow and ball lightning) to the extreme are bringing us full circle. In fact, weather is about the only category of news the shameless mainstream media has consistently down played in the past years.

Reporting bad weather has become synonymous with a slow news day.

And so The Great Blizzard of 2011 was kind of sort of a non-event (unless you were in it). All things being equal, the mainstream national media would surely have jumped at the chance to point out that there was a storm raging on Earth that was the same size as Jupiter's Great Red Spot. That's dramatic! That's sensational! That's ratings!

But things are not equal.

Any reasonable Jovian looking down on the Earth would see that peculiar forces at work on our Tiny Blue Spot as surely as we can see that their Great Red Spot is nothing to sneeze at.

So why can't we see that when we turn the telescopes on ourselves? Why aren't we putting the onus on the media to connect the dots?

◇

On the very day the blizzard raged in the Northern Hemisphere, half a world away, in Australia—a continent at the time already afflicted with severe flooding—was pummeled by a tropical cyclone that also rated as "one of the biggest in history."

When viewed in a larger context, these aren't separate storms, but parts of a larger whole, a global system, a pattern shouting at us, 'Hey look at me!,' a pattern we need desperately to see emerging.

There sure does seem to be a lot of things that are the "biggest ever recorded" coming round recently. Seems that American French Fries and SUVs aren't the only things we like supersized.

High fructose corn syrup can now be labeled simply "corn sugar." A friendly name—the same way we name our storms Hurricane Harriet instead of Hurricane Hitler.

I suppose one big thing deserves another.

But no matter how much wind you blow, you'll never convince me the biggest SUVs in history don't have a hand to play in the formation of the biggest storms in history.

Oh, sigh. Global Warming, again? Really? That is so 2000s. I thought we killed that foolish idea once and for all with the 2010 elections in which every single newly elected Republican congressman publicly confirmed that global warming was a hoax.

◇

To settle the matter once and for all, let's take a page from the FDA guidebook.

Recently, the American Corn Farmers Coalition (there's an American Corn Farmers Coalition? You betcha!) whinnied and whined to the FDA that high fructose corn syrup had gotten

The Jovian view of Earth

What's going on with the Tiny Blue Spot?

I'd hate to be having the weather they're having.

a bad wrap. And like a suburban soccer mom with the spoiled children riding in back of the super-sized SUV watching a DVD to keep them silent, the FDA agreed with the Corn Famers Coalition that the words 'high fructose corn syrup' sure had gotten some unfavorably bad media play of late. How dare they say high fructose corn syrup is a silent killer that causes obesity? That's just sensationalism! And it's outrageous. And we won't stand for it.

And then finally, the day we had all hoped for so long would eventually arrive, did—the day the words high fructose corn syrup would be forever banned from supermarket shelves across America.

In almost every other country on Earth, high fructose corn syrup is illegal. Outlawed. A toxic chemical.

People used to pay attention when 100-year floods occurred, because, as the name implies, they only happened once every 100 years. Not anymore.

In late 2010, in the ye ole freedom-loving US of A, under the protective auspices of the government and its ongoing mission to look out for corporations' best interests, the FDA sided with the Corn Farmers Coalition. Henceforth, did that agency decree, all traces of high fructose corn syrup contained in any foods sold in America could knowingly and willfully be relabeled "corn sugar."

A much friendlier name without all that nasty bad publicity.

◇

It's the same way we name our biggest storms. We use the friendliest, nurturing, motherly names we can imagine like Hurricane Harriet and Denise and Susanne... not Hurricane Hitler or Cyclone Caesar.

What harm could possible come from Harriet, Denise or Susanne? I once had a date with a girl named Susanne. As I remember, she stood me up. I think I'll wait around and see if she shows up this time.

So, if "high fructose corn syrup" simply has gotten a bad rap, and changing the name will solve all our problems, perhaps "global warming" just ended up with a bad reputation because all those scientists in the pockets of the oil companies kept insisting it was a hoax.

So, let's not say global warming ever again. Case settled.

Heaven knows we need to stop all this name-calling anyway. So I won't say "high fructose corn syrup" and you don't have to say "global warming."

Instead, let me put it this way. The current storm of "biggest-ever-in-history" storms storming the planet is caused by the following:

10% to 15% more moisture in the atmosphere.

Which is caused by the following:

Rainforests are being cut at an alarming rate, which leaves less green leaves to absorb water from the atmosphere and return it to the water table. Instead, moisture remains in the atmosphere until it comes down as, you guessed it, Tropical Drink Tammy served with one of those cute little umbrellas. At the same time, there's more new water entering the atmosphere all the time because those dang icecaps just keep melting. And what happens to melted ice? Well, some of it becomes water straightaway that causes the sea-level to rise and flooding to occur. And some of the ice merely evaporates into the atmosphere and comes down as yet another huge storm.

We need to stop all this name-calling. I won't say "high fructose corn syrup" and you don't have to say "global warming."

Just Google "flooding"+ "current year" + "your hometown."

Ironically, the thing that used to make people pay attention when 100-year floods occurred is that, as the name implies, they only occur once every 100 years.

Today, 100-year floods happen every year. Sometimes twice in the same year. Like the record-breaking tsunami in Japan last March that broke the record of the record-breaking tsunami in Japan last February, both of which were dwarfed by the tsunami that broke the nuclear power plant.

I would like to issue this challenge:

I would truly like to know if anyone can find any mainstream media outlet who asks a weatherman on-the-record, "So, Mr. Weather Personality, about this major blizzard in Chicago and the devastating cyclone in Australia that are happening on the same day. Is there any possibility these aren't isolated incidents? Could they possibly be related? And if so, what's causing all this? Can you connect the dots for us?"

You may find some conjecture on some blog. Or a Google search might turn up some secret Wikileaks document. But I have never heard any major meteorological indictment made in the mainstream media. I might even settle for a tabloid. Even that would be something.

Somewhere beneath the huge 50 point headline, "Regis Dying: Real Reason he Retied!" and then the 8 point subhead "Friends Fear," I'd like to see some blazingly large type proclaiming, "Connection between flooding, blizzards and cyclones spotted!"

Even if it does come with the microscopic disclaimer, "by Jovian space alien looking through telescope."

◇

And stay tuned. Our weather is cyclical. Each winter, the cycle begins all over again. If we have severe snowfall one winter, we're going to see severe flooding that spring. And more liquid water ending up in the oceans raises sea level, also helping to raise the overall temperature of the oceans over the summer months. Which translated into more melting of the polar ice sheets. Talk about a cliff hanger.

Be sure to tune in next season.

An Earth for An Earth

One of the crucial ingredients to any successful television show is the necessity for each episode, each dramatic event to be bigger, better, more dramatic than the last. More and more drama is always required in order to get the same rise out of people. Television inevitably creates a sense of viewer apathy. Now that you've seen blood-and-guts, the next time you see them won't carry the same shock value with it. You'll need more blood, more guts. It's an endless spiral, the dog chasing its tail. How much will be enough? Well, it depends on how much you had last time.

Last season's cliff hanger about the Great White Spot set the stage for this year's season premier, the biggest spring melt and flooding in the history of the Midwest.

Given all this, it seem to me that global warming would be the biggest hit reality show of the millennia. It seems to be a story line made for T.V—more and more dramatic events every season, higher and higher death tolls, bigger and bigger special effects to wow the viewing public.

Last season's cliff hanger, about the Great White Spot set the stage for this year's season premier, the biggest spring melt and flooding in the history of the Midwest. Rivers overflowed their banks, communities were evacuated, waterways were re-directed to flood smaller communities in order to save bigger cities from flooding.

Spring floods and winter storms are undeniably connected. And the scope of devastation is increasing with each new calamity.

Now in its 46th year, this is the oldest reality show around—

almost rivaling NBC's longest-runing soap opera. (It's been in
the lives of many Americans five-days every week since 1965).

The term global warming can be traced back to a 1975
in paper by Wally Broecker published in the journal *Science*
called "Are we on the brink of a pronounced global warming?
That was one of the landmark papers published in a major science
journal directly linking human technology and climate change.
It's been in the lives of all Americans ever since (and long before
it was officially discovered—since the first day we burned the
first drop of oil).

Compared with the latest studies about how plants
need sunlight, few news outlets give the microphone
to experts who study Global Warming.

So why aren't more people tuning into the made-for-TV Global
Warming series? I believe it's the way it's being covered. Broad-
casters are choosing to evoke the power of viewer apathy from
the media, rather than its power to shock and awe us into action.

Every evening on the news we should be hearing about the
latest findings from the University of Your Home State, reporting that changes in climate are caused by ...., or we can expect
the ongoing trend to be....

But we don't hear things like that regularly. We do if we
search them out amid a lot of sound and furry from across the
political isle.

Compared with the latest studies debunking everything from
vitamins and minerals to fresh water, the loud-mouthed experts
are relatively mute on the national stage when it comes to Global
Warming. Few news outlets are brave enough to give them the
microphone.

At best, they'll tease you about the weather, promo-ing some
dramatic images of tsunamis and the like, promising a story after
the commercial break.

Too often , there is no story. There are just more dramatic

images. And a voice over saying something along the lines of, "Seems like there's been a lot of unusual weather this year." And then something vague like, "Seems like no one knows what to expect next."

The apathetic main-stream reporting carries the undercurrent, "There, there, little children, don't worry. It'll be okay."

The specific "report" I'm referring to above aired on CBS' Sunday Morning show, the same show that regularly gives Ben Stein a podium to rant about how society is threatening to "punish" rich people by its desire raise their taxes.

When Stein's editorial ran as well as when that charade about the water aired, I called into the station's extremely-hard-to-fund viewer hot line to complain. Phone lines were jammed in both cases, and CBS ran a timid follow up the following week, essentially saying "We're sorry [our viewers don't agree with us.]"

Networks' official stance is that the content of their broadcasts doesn't reflect the opinion of the station or its owners. And certainly not that of its viewers. So if nobody agrees with what's being aired, why is it?

The vast majority of calls, CBS had the decency to report next week to give the air of objectivity, "disagreed with Ben Stein."

That was putting it mildly. The tone of all the web-based hate-mail out there was more like, "You're not being punished. It's evening the playing field! But even if you *are* being punished, you deserve it, you spoiled brats!"

Of course, all networks' official stance is that the content of their broadcasts doesn't reflect the opinion of the station or its owners.

Certainly not of its viewers, I would add.

But if nobody agrees with what's being aired, why is it being aired?

It's gross malfeasance of the national media to say the least.

In a courtroom, lawyers will often state "facts" that are inadmissible, which the judge will promptly declare, "Strike that from the record!"

Yet the statement is out there to influence the jury. It can't simply be erased from their minds. Even if we don't believe any of the reports we hear, the fact is, we keep listening to them. And soon enough, we believe what we hear if we hear it often enough.

◇

We're shown dramatic images, which serve ultimately to de-sesitize us all. When one million people die in September, it doesn't seem very shocking because 750 thousand died in August. In fact, if only 500 thousand die next October, that would be a slow news day.

The media should be connecting the dots. Demanding answers. Interviewing experts. Editorializing in the fashion of Woodward and Bernstein whose undercover reporting exposed the Watergate Scandal in 1974. But it's not.

The media is reporting the news as it happens in a parallel universe, a magical place down the rabbit hole called the water world of corporate media.

And viewer apathy sets in.

The only news we're getting comes from a parallel universe, a magical place down the rabbit hole known as the water world of corporate media.

Global warming is a ghost in our cultural closet. Maybe if we don't admit its there it will just go away.

There's only one explanation why the news media appears to be asleep on the job. They've gotten a "promotion" from media outlet to entertainment show, which comes with a much bigger paycheck signed by corporate America.

Corporations are as worried about global warming just as the rest of us are. But there's something else they're even more worried about … taking the blame.

Corporations will never publicly admit the problem exists, because that means they might just be fingered for causing it. No one wants to be the fall guy for this one. They might get sued!

Don't admit cigarettes cause cancer. Don't admit Co2 causes global warming. Deny, deny, deny.

There's only explanation why the news media appears to be sleeping on the job. They've gotten a "promotion" from media outlet to entertainment shows, which comes with a bigger paycheck signed by corporate America.

It's the height of absurdity that anyone is worried about getting sued for causing global warming. Or that anyone's even thinking about trying to sue anyone for causing global warming.

I propose that the UN or some other global body offers *carte-de-blanche* amnesty for any corporation that admits global warming exists and that it was their practices, be it fossil fuel-related, agriculturally related or anything else,which caused the problem.

Someone has to admit the problem exists before we can all ban together and start seriously searching for the solution. I believe that when we get down to the business of changing our ways, corporations will even find it very profitable. As profitable as re-tooling America to enter World War II. As profitable as building the electrical grid so electricity could be sold everywhere.

We're talking about completely re-tooling society and infrastructure. That's a lot of work. And a lot of work means a lot of profit. And the one thing everyone's worried about: jobs.

We just have to put aside our fear of change, and have the tiniest bit of vision in a long-term plan. There's plenty of work to do, and plenly of people to do it.

It can only begin when we admit we're facing a problem so severe, so threatening to all life on Earth, that inaction could cause the extinction of our species and plenty of others.

Dreaming up cruel and unusual punishments for whoever's

responsible is absurd. Sure they could all be charged for crimes against humanity (and ecology) but the only good that the fear of punishment will do is keep the Powers that Be motivated to keep the truth buried.

Unless global warming was caused by aliens, and we put a lien on their home world, there is no possibility for revenge here. Except the one Earth takes out on humanity.

This isn't a problem you can prosecute anyone for. We need to put aside our lust for revenge this one time. The 'eye for an eye' mentality is useless here. What would it even mean in this case—an Earth for an Earth? Unless global warming was caused by aliens, and we put a lien on their home world, there is no possibility for revenge here. We're all in this together

Unless we admit the problem soon, there will be revenge, on a global scale. Revenge is a dish best served cold, a lesson we will learn the hard way when Earth strikes back by getting rid of us once and for all by beginning the next ice age.

It's well within her power to do it. She's been far too patient with us so far.

The Albinos

If the Great Flood was intended to wipe the slate clean when we'd gone so far off track, our "fresh start" doesn't seem to have produced much better results this time around.

The Flood has almost as much historical and mythological significance as a metaphorical relationship to the tide of human events.

Indeed, the re-surgence of civilization after the historical great flood marked the beginning of The Great Flood of Western Thought.

> Albinism is associated with a number of vision defects, including astigmatism and myopia. No wonder the Western world view is so skewed. We see what we want to see and our stigmas are largely irrational.

It's been during the 8,000 years since that the world has experienced the meteoric rise of Western Culture when a small group of albinos rose up and re-created the world in their own image.

That's a bit odd, don't you think? For one small group of genetically mutated naked apes to do all that? It was their belief, their expectation that 'might meant right' that allowed the minority to feel justified in enslaving all of nature. It all comes down to a single, false expectation about the way the world should be.

The unashamed, unabashed, ruthless rule of Western Thought has remorselessly bleached the world. Albinism is associated with a number of vision defects, including astigmatism. No wonder the Western world view is so skewed. We see what we want to see and our stigmas are largely irrational.

They Day They Took Kodachrome Away

Take a snapshot at this moment in history and it looks pretty monochromatic. Even Paul Simon's favorite Kodachrome film couldn't give us back those nice bright colors or those greens of summer.

Everything looks worse in black and white, or in this case through the lens of a monochromatic culture. Think about the crops we grow, corn and potatoes and apples for instance. Once hundreds of varieties grew wild, even thousands. From those we have trimmed back and now raise only a handful of domesticated varieties—the ones we like best. Putting the lie to the claim that we like diversity. We don't.

Pick your poison. As corporations manufacture the same products for global distribution, they dump the same chemicals into the water supply everywhere.

Sadly, our culture is the same as our crops. On the surface, one of the most obvious symptoms is mass-retail-chain-psychosis. You can buy the same products for the same price anywhere in the Western world (and in many of our former colonies). Speaking from personal experience, there's a Wal-Club-Mart-Shop-Company equivalent in the second and third worlds.

Fourty-four countries have a Wal-Club-Mart-Shop-Company of their own, easily making this trend one of the frontrunners in global homogenization.

Pick your poison. As they manufacture the same products for global distribution, they dump the same chemicals into the water supply everywhere.

But let's stay a little closer to home, where many of the Mega-merchants are based. These conglomerates have their home bases right here in the United Corporations of America, from which they plan and execute the logistics of world domination (and homogenization).

Looking deeper than surface symptoms, we see that it's not just the commercial landscape of the Earth that's flat, but people's lives as well.

Farmer or rocket scientist or coal miner, all careers
share the same fundamental responsibility:
to make money for someone else.

And not just the lives of the individuals in the current generation, but the lives of their parents and their parents as well. Here in the United Corporations of America, the vast majority of us have all had pretty much the same career for the past 150 years or so (since the Industrial Devolution).

That career has many different categories, but it's all the same work—from assembly line worker, to secretaries, to marketing professionals to railroad worker to farmer.

If you work on an assembly line, its immaterial whether your line produces automobiles, whiskey, Styrofoam plates, herbicides, crayons or newspapers. Your job is to work in a mass production facility, making as many widgets as possible each and every day.

Secretaries may work for company X or company Y and have wide-ranging responsibilities, even changing throughout the centuries as one technology fad gives way to another. Answering phones becomes answering e-mail, typewriters become computers.

Just as the product you make on the line is immaterial and who's phone you answer is irrelevant, whether you're a farmer or a "professional" or an engineer, all careers share the same fundamental responsibility: to make money for someone else.

There are a few hundred thousand someone-else's, and a few hundred million people working for someone else's. Your career, should you choose to pursue one, is to make money for the guy standing on the top of the pyramid.

Even more mind-boggling is that if you're reading this and you're between the ages of 20-50 (the middle of the bell-shaped population curve—and that's a pretty big range considering what I'm going to say next), then the odds are at least one of your four grandparents worked in at least one of the following environments at some time in their life: department store, factory, mine or farm.

The grandparents of all 300 million Americans
alive today all held one of four jobs.

That's a rather broad statement, isn't it? The grandparents of all 300 million Americans alive today all had one of four jobs.

Gone are the days when your parents' parents' had a particular trade. A blacksmith had a very different life from a cobbler from a mason from a glass blower from a farmer. Today, all of those separate professions have been steam rolled together under the umbrella of mass production.

Forget the land of opportunity where anyone can be whatever they want to be. Regardless of what you're doing or making, it's the same job.

Not to say there aren't individuals who still perform those jobs. But by far the vast majority of these tasks are performed by huge staffs at mass-production laboratories.

And your parents' generation had an even more homogenized experience than their parents. Odds are more than even that if you're reading this and are between the ages of 20-50, at least one of your parents worked with one of these *two* things: mechanical tools or electrical devises.

It's even worse now. *All* work today, is done either partly or completely with the aid of a computer.

Computers employ more people than any single industry in the history of history.

Architects used to sit at drafting tables and perform fine measurements with tools.

Cartographers drew maps.

Newspaper men did "paste-up."
Writers wrote with pen and paper.
Engineers designed real-world models.
Chemists combined combustible materials in a lab.

Today, computers employee people. We all work
for our computers. Do computers help us,
or do we help computers?

Astronomers gazed into telescopes and made meticulous measurements.

Paul Simon's Kodachrome was developed in a dark room.

Recording artists worked with 8-tracks.

Film editors spliced film together.

All of this now, all of it, is done while sitting behind a monitor, in front of a keyboard at a desk.

There are still miners, there are still doctors, there are still construction workers, there are still plumbers.

But for every worker who's actually laying bricks today or cleaning pipes, there are 1-2 of him sitting in an office somewhere behind a monitor, in front of a keyboard and at a desk.

Behind every line worker and very doctor there are office jobs and support staff. The health insurance industry employs more office workers than hospitals do doctors.

This is the homogenization of experience, the homogenization of life. And it paints a rather bleak picture. White-washed office walls, white noise and computer screens are the antithesis of those nice bright colors and those greens of summer. No one will look back on history as a sunny day. Unless, of course, things get far, far worse in the not-so far-off future.

So, then, as your grandparents all worked one of four jobs, and your parents one of two, what will your grandsons and granddaughters say about you?

They will say precisely this: my grandparents, all four of them!, all did exactly the same thing: they were slaves to their computer.

Pavlov's Humans

The Russian psychologist Ivan Pavlov showed that dogs will begin to develop rituals to exert control.

In his experiments, Pavlov rings a bell (or a wide variety of other stimuli, including electric shock) just before feeding his dogs, thus teaching them to associate that stimulus with food.

After the conditioning firmly takes root, the next stage of the experiment is to give the stimulus without food. At first the dogs are probably just disappointed (I don't know; I can't read a dog's mind).

Sometimes observing the observer tells us more than observing the observed.

At some arbitrarily later time, they are fed without the stimulus to announce dinner.

As the experiment is repeated, sometimes food appearing at the sound of a bell, sometimes not, the dogs begin to perform what can only be described as rituals.

Some begin to walk around in circles, clockwise, counterclockwise, wag their tail, bark exactly four times. Every dog in the study developed its own arbitrary, ritualistic behavior, but each successive time, the ritualistic behavior became more and more eccentric.

By doing this, they were (Pavlov said) trying to exert control over the appearance of food which was no longer predictable

Was control actually their motivation for walking around in circles? I still can't read the minds of dogs.

Whether the dogs were actually trying to exert control, we know for sure that's the motivation Pavlov projected onto them. Sometimes observing the observer tells us more than observing the observed.

Pavlov *needed* to figure out why these dogs were walking in circles. Whether he was right or not is beside the point. He needed to explain it—understand the results of his experiments. Not knowing means being out of control, and that is utterly unacceptable to humans.

Our need to know, to control, is very rare in the mind of living beings. It is a bizarre eccentricity.

The Law of Entropy

Our great eccentricity rooted in the need for control led us to build great churches and cathedrals. (God will favor the congregation with the largest one, don't you know.)

And so as we build ever taller, we find we must develop new architectural techniques. First comes the arch. Then we connect a series of arches together along an axis, and thus invent the vault.

And we forge a chain of always-increasingly complex links (eccentricities).

These same eccentricities led the Egyptians to shave their heads (to control fleas). Of course the flees just moved further ... um ... south. I'd prefer them on my head myself.

Now their bald heads were becoming sunburned by the heat of the scorching desert. So they started wearing wigs. But wigs can transmit lice, too. (Just as kids today can spread lice by wearing each other's baseball caps). But no matter, wigs grew from (semi)practical things into a fashion statement.

Our desire to exert control is ultimately fruitless. It always is.

It always leads to more and more and more eccentric behaviors, inventions and technologies that are each more uncontrollable than the last.

<><

The Law of Entropy is a scientific principle that says: the universe is always becoming more and more disordered.

Break a glass and you end up with into a million sharp pieces in a disordered mess on the floor.

The mess has more *entropy* than the glass did when in was still in one, simple, smooth piece.

And you'll never see those million pieces spontaneously come back together again and re-form into a glass. In other words, the entropy of the universe *never* decreases. It always increases. Always becomes more disordered.

> Every problem we face today is a thousand times
> knottier than any problem we faced 200 years ago.

That's the very reason why human control over the world is necessary. Our lives, our civilization, is based on the notion that we must create order from chaos. (And the belief that we can.)

Nature is unpredictable. But We can conquer it.

Let's start farming. Straight rows of crops laid out in a grid is far more ordered than a native prairie or a primaeval forest.

We can cultivate the land, farm it, control it, bring order to the chaos. Wait, there's a problem. Pests kill our crops. Stupid, unpredictable, chaotic nature! No matter! We'll make chemical pesticides and bring order to the chaos by killing all the pests.

Every problem in the world is an example of disorder. Every solution we create is an example of us bringing order to the chaos.

By making order from chaos, we create civilization. Civilization is: human ingenuity bringing order to chaos.

Let's pave smooth roads, let's build bridges, canals, tame the world, create order from the chaos of nature.

Human civilization is the only thing in the universe not subject to the law of entropy.

We alone don't have to play by the rules.

Right?

◇

Problem.

It seems that every solution we come up always poses another, bigger, more complicated problem. At which point, we invent a new, more complicated technology to solve the new problem. Which creates another problem ... on so on.

We layer solution after solution after solution upon each other.

Let's take a step back and look at the complicated, vast, sprawling, tangled web of civilization we've created around us.

Every problem we face today is a thousand times knottier than any problem we faced 200 years ago. The entropy of civilization is always increasing, never decreasing. Things never get simpler.

It's much more complicated to repair a digital watch than a grandfather clock. It's much more complicated to repair a grand-father clock than a sundial.

We think the construction of our civilization is a force that controls the chaos of the universe, controls entropy.

But complexity arises from simplicity. Always.

But disorder (complexity) arises from order (simplicity). Always.

That's why every new problem is always more complex than the last.

With each new thing we create in order to exert control over disorder, to make sense out of chaos, we create an ever increasingly complex, dis-ordered system which we call civilization.

Civilization does not exercise power over the law of entropy.

It's subject to the law just like anything else.

Half Full? Half Empty? Safe to Drink?

The next time someone accuses you—or you accuse someone else—of having a glass is half empty kind of attitude, remember that it's irrelevant whether the glass is half full or brimming over the top if that water's unsafe to drink.

And if we're talking about bottled water, is it really just tap water in a fancy BPA container? And can you find traces of every pharmaceutical known to man swimming in the mix, as is the case in most municipal tap water?

And if it's bottled spring water, has it been stolen from a spring "purchased" by a corporation for next to nothing. Is the corporation now sucking water out of the stream at such a rate that the agricultural lands it used to irrigate are now experiencing drought-like conditions?

And if it's well-water, does it come from a rural area where fraking has contaminated the water table and natural gas has leached into the drinking water? If you hold a match over your half-full/empty cup, will you ignite a fireball?

If your glass is half full, did you realize there are places in rural Africa where it's been made illegal for local villages to drill their own wells? And wells that have existed for generations are filled with concrete for "public health considerations" because corporate interests have polluted the water supply. Now, locals are forced to buy water from those very same corporations, when the water had been free, fresh and crystal clear since before anyone can remember, before the 1980s.

Who cares how full your glass is. Can you drink the water?

Eat No Evil

Ingredients: castoreum, ammonium sulfate, natural color, carmine, carminic acid, lanolin, L-cysteine, cystine, allura, allura red AC, rennet, silicon dioxide, hydrolyzed vegetable protein, aginomoto, Accent, Natural Meat Tenderizer, monosodium glutamate (MSG), corn sugar, aspartame.

You need to bring a dictionary with you every time you go to the grocery store. Luckily, I've put one together for you:

Castoreum - beaver anal glands
Ammonium sulfate – fertilizer
Carmine or Carminic acid – crushed bugs as red food coloring
Natural color – crushed bugs as red food coloring
Lanolin – sheep sweat
L-cysteine and/or Cystine – human hair and/or duck feathers
Allura and/or Allura Red AC – coal tar
Rennet – the fourth stomach of a young cow
Silicon dioxide – sand
Corn sugar – high fructose corn syrup
Hydrolyzed Vegetable Protein – MSG
Aginomoto – MSG
Accent - MSG
Natural Meat Tenderizer – MSG

And just what is MSG anyway? Oh, don't be silly! It's just salt. Salt mixed with glutamate. The real question is, what is glutamate?

Gultemamte, along with it's buddy, aspartate (think the artificial sweetener) is an "excitotoxin" naturally occurring in humans who have suffered severe brain damage. And it's not something you want to be eating.

You might not think about it, but restaurants use these ingredients, too, and not just fast food chains. Steak houses.

Darden Restaurants is a public ally traded company on the NYSE. Their three most popular brands are a steak house, a sea food restaurant and an Italian restaurant. Like "salt" and "glutamate," Publicly Traded Restaurant are words that simply should not be next to each other in a sentence.

I've always read labels. If I can't pronounce it, I don't buy it. Today I'm doing so even more diligently, and abiding by this golden rule: if it doesn't grow in the ground, don't eat it. That's really what the whole "Raw food" idea breaks down to in its simplest form.

The only meals I've skipped are ones at restaurants.
The only food I've given up is Soylent Green.

The only difference in my diet today is that I Eat No Evil. I'm down 45 lbs. There are no side effects. The only meals I've skipped are ones at restaurants. The only food I've given up is Soylent Green.

Last night I ate double-chocolate chip ice cream. The night before I enjoyed chocolate chip cookies. For dinner, honey butter glazed sweet potatoes. Tortilla soup the night before. All made with 100% raw ingredients! Nothing processed, nothing gained.

And just in case you think that sounds like getting too "creative," you should see all the things they're doing with corn these days.

Now that's getting creative.

All The Nutrition Your Body Needs...

Remember the television ads for "Total" with the magically appearing bowls of breakfast cereal?

The voice over proclaimed, "You would need this many servings of the leading competitor" —queue the magically appearing bowls of cereal, stacking themselves up behind the un-expecting not-a-morning-person sitting at the breakfast table—"in order to get all nutrition you get from one bowl of Total! A single serving of Total Complete provides 100% of the daily vitamins and minerals your body needs!"

And poof, the 12-story stack of cereal bowls reduces to just a single bowl, and our not-a-morning-person suddenly peps up and is much relieved.

Fast forward into the future a dozen or so years.

Today the voice over proclaims, "You would need this many servings of fruit and vegetables" —queue the magically appearing veggies (arugula and collard greens and chicories and kohlrabi and kale, oh my!) stacking themselves up behind the un-expecting not-a-vegetarian sitting at the dinner table—"in order to get all calories you get from just a one tablespoon of high fructose corn syrup! A single serving of high fructose corn syrup provides 100% of the daily caloric intake your body needs!"

Have Your Desktop Cleared Off
By The End Of The Decade

I've been reading articles from various sources about all the new "Pads" either already available or poised to strike soon. Every tech company seems to be developing one.

Everyday there's less and less a desktop computer can do that an iPad or similar can't. Apps are getting more and more "full scale." Did you know you can now edit movies (in full HD) and process photos (jpegs and RAW) on iPad apps? You can publish e-magazines with software very similar to Adobe's InDesign. You can take notes during business meetings or write in your journal on an iPad with a digital pen that interfaces with the touch screen (and can recognize your bad handwriting).

More and more iPad apps are even being programmed on iPads themselves.

What can't an iPad do? What will it be able to do a year from now? In five years? A decade from now we'll look back and say, "I can't believe people used to have desktop computers! Geez, those things were dinosaurs!"

The biggest stumbling block that remains before that brave new world is ushered in seems to be the lack of a single, unified operating system across the mobile industry.

Will it be Mac OS or Web OS? Or even Windows??? (Not windows, please no more windows! Show windows the door).

Whoever ekes it out, I believe it will be decided sooner than we think. Or maybe all apps simply become cross-platform. Think back oh so long ago to the 1990's (20 years ago!) when Macs and PCs were still dueling it out for the honor to sit upon the thrown high atop your desk.

Today the mobile internet has made those old clunky desktop computers look like Humpty Dumpty sitting way up there.

At present, there is no clear-cut choice for one single OS in the mobile marketplace. But as soon as a frontrunner emerges, "Have your desk cleared out by the end of the week" is going to take on a whole new meaning.

Where have all the hippies gone?

That's the question Peter, Paul and Mary neglected to ask in their ballad, "Where have all the Flowers Gone?"

Hippies, you see, wanted to change the world. They didn't really have a clear vision of what they wanted to change it into, which was part of the downfall of the movement. They only knew they wanted it to change.

When the movement died or individuals burned-out on LSD or too-few results, and the financiers of Woodstock ended up lost in legal battles contesting who was to blame for the most successful free music concert in the world, a great light went out.

But the spirit didn't. Hippies still wanted to change the world.

Now they would do so by changing people's minds, not the scene. Free concerts failing, they would now promote and advertise them.

> Who would hire a marketing professional,
> whether he wore a tie or tie-dye?

Many ex-hippies went into the profession they believed had the most power and influence to change the world and people's minds: marketing.

They are and always have been the creative types. They had the drive to think the thoughts that could change the world.

Then they tried to mass-market them.

But if they went into marketing, or started their own agencies, who were they working for? Who would hire a marketing professional, whether he wore a tie or tie-dye?

Corporate America, who, too, wanted to change society into

material slaves living in a material world.

So in one of ironies's quirkier turns, the creative hippies who wanted to change the world and overthrow corporate control ended up feeding the very beast they set out to starve.

Where have all the hippies gone? Gone to Corporate America (almost) every one.

Who Has the Monopoly On You?

I'm going to tell you about the absolute best product to hit the marketplace this year. No, this century. In fact, in all of human history! It will change your life. And it retails for an unbelievably low price! You're not going to believe your eyes.

You want to know what it is, no doubt. But wait. First let me tell you what it can do! This product has everything! This product is as essential as the air you breathe! This product will feed your entire family and put a roof over their heads. In fact, without this product, your family will very likely starve to death. Once you see what this amazing item is, I'm sure you'll agree, you won't be able to live without it.

But good news, we do offer an affiliate program. More on that later.

Alright, so what is it, you ask? Is it the latest plastic widget worth all of about 5 cents manufactured in Bangladesh and sold by telemarketers in India? Is it the best as-seen-on TV product ever? Does it have an incredibly low, low price tag of just $19.95?

Any guesses? Anyone? A rubber snuggy? Rubber snuggy you're the one. You make bath time oh so … profitable?

No, no, it's not a rubber snuggy! And it's not sold on TV. It's not even available in stores. In fact, we have patented this amazing technology! It's only available through us! We have the exclusive monopoly on it.

So what is? The suspense is over.

It's you. If you work for a corporation, it has the exclusive monopoly on you!

Your talents, your gifts, everything you have to offer (professionally) is monopolized by your company.

Do you think the brilliant person who patents ingenious ideas while working for a corporation keeps those patent rights? Oh no. The corporation does. It holds the intellectual copyrights to everything you may have thought of or invented while working there.

If you work for a corporation, it has the exclusive monopoly on you!

Most employment contracts include non-compete clauses, too. So should you ever wish to leave your company, you are legally banned from offering your services to any of its competitors for years. Your company has registered an extended patent license on you.

So not only does your company have the monopoly on you, as well as all the copyrights you come with, it also owns exclusive patent rights that won't expire for years!

The moral of the story: Every skill you have been hired for, ever skill a company is willing to pay you for, is marketable! In fact, your skills and abilities are very valuable. So valuable that you can't simply work for the company. Oh no. It's your company now. It owns you. It retains exclusive access to your skills!

So how much are your exclusive rights worth to you? Is it the same they're worth to the company? Surely not. But since it's a monopoly, your company sets the price.

You've only been hired to do the job you're doing because your company knows it can make more money from your talents than the salary it's paying you.

You're their best selling product.

But wait! There's more!

If, while you're working for them, your unique talents and gifts happen to land your company more business than they had before you came along, you might even get a bonus!

A bonus, really? It's a commission! You're earning a sales commission on your own abilities — the things you have been able to do for your company. And all you get for your hard work is a lousy commission — sorry, a bonus. Wait, a bonus!? That sounds like you're getting something extra. Something more than you deserve.

You are the best product the company has ever had. And it does think of you as a product. Human capital, it calls you. Incidentally, we're told that corporations are thought of as people by the Supreme Court.

Corporations even have something they like to call "peasant insurance." They collect big in the "unfortunate" event you should die while working for them.

Make no mistake, you are very marketable. So marketable that the savvy capitalists have realized they can sell you at a huge premium. They've even set-up an affiliate program – a pyramid scheme – to re-sell you. You are your own affiliate, selling yourself and getting a commission from the sale.

We all know how pyramid schemes work. The first ones in, the guys at the top, make out like gang busters.

And you, the last one into the Ponzi scheme — how does it end for you?

Well, a few corporations even have something they like to call peasant insurance – an insurance policy they have taken out on you. They collect – and collect big – in the "unfortunate" event you should die while working for them. It doesn't even have to be at work. You just have to die at any point under any circumstances before you leave. Or are terminated. Or downsized. Or Indianized.

And the money from the peasant insurance? It certainly doesn't go to your family. It goes to your company.

So act now! This is one amazing money-back guarantee you can't afford to miss!

See how millions of people are already living the life they've dreamed. And it all begins when you pick up that phone and become one of our affiliated partners.

Buy into this once-in-a-lifetime opportunity and start selling yourself short today.

Always practice safe shopping

*W*ith *the economy* still in its "kick me while I'm down" stupor, shopping at dollar stores has been on the rise, and the trend is being reported by the mainstream media.

I've often wondered, how the heck does it make sense for dollar stores to sell products for, well, $1? And why then are these same products retailing for exponential multiples in grocery stores across the U.S.? Dollar stores just don't add up.

The answer came in the most unlikely of places, while I was abroad in the third world.

The truth (about big business) is stranger than fiction.

I lived in Africa for two years serving as an International Volunteer for an organization I cannot disclose in a country I cannot reveal, due to the same muzzle laws that landed Oprah in a whole bunch of manure in Texas.

But what I can say is this: Living in the third world, and seeing American products on grocery stores shelves, I was wan to ask, "Hey, what is this Brand-That-Must-Not-Be-Named of paper towels doing here?"

A high ranking official, we'll call him Deep Bargain, launched into a big long explanation. I was sorry I asked, enlightened and frightened all at the same time.

The truth (about big business) is stranger than fiction.

The following applies to some, not all, of Dollar Store merchandise:

American dollar stores re-sell goods in the American market that were slated for sale in the third-world. These goods were produced overseas. (Isn't everything?) Yes, but when manufactured for a third-world market, U.S. product standards don't apply. Third-world versions of American products are inferior to their American-market counterparts—even though, in some cases, the two versions of the same product are produced in the same plant (usually in China).

I've often wondered, how the heck does it make sense for dollar stores to sell products for, well, $1?

I'll share one example. Free condoms were distributed by Americans in the third-world country where I lived. These came from two different batches. One batch was reserved for U.S. Volunteers. The other batch was only to be distributed to the Malagasy people, and Deep Secret warned us, "Don't use these yourself. These aren't reliable. They break more often than not."

What??? We're here in Africa trying (among other things) to stop the spread of HIV by knowingly passing out defective condoms, thus instilling a false sense of security in the Malagasy people which will ultimately lead to an increase in the spread of HIV? What? Huh? Say that again?

Rant over. Back on point. If the goods manufactured for the third-world don't sell in the intended market (there can be a number of different reasons for this) the American company ships the remaining product back to the U.S. and distributes it to Dollar Stores practically (sometimes literally) for free. Dollar stores are "where products go to die," not to sound overly dramatic or anything.

American dollar stores re-sell goods in the American market that were slated for sale in the third-world.

When America is a "secondary market," U.S. product standards don't apply. The thinking is, the primary market standards will always be higher than the secondary market standards, thus creating a loophole that dollar stores have stepped into. This applies most often to things like paper towels, dish washing detergent, etc. Nonconsumables.

Yet, paradoxically, some products seem more economical to buy at grocery stores than at dollar stores. Yes, thankfully. Even in the secondary market, some products (mostly foodstuffs) must still meet U.S. safety standards.

So the next time you see your favorite brand of dish washing detergent on sale for 1/5 the price you're used to paying, ask why.

Does that $1 bottle really have the same, salmonella-repelling, bovine-spongiform-encephalopathy-killing (mad cow disease), germ fighting power as a $5 bottle?

I don't know. And I don't want to learn the hard way.

Always practice safe shopping.

A Cynicism Born of Capitalism

*E*ver *notice how* so many items ring up at the wrong price?

Ever notice how many items are on sale everywhere you shop? These two things are connected I believe

Those sale prices are the real prices, you realize. If you ever buy anything full price.... well, P.T. Barnum said it best: "There's a sucker born every minute."

The widely misquoted Carl Marx is believed to have said, "A capitalist will sell you the rope to hang himself with."

That implies a cynicism about capitalism, but also an irony that Capitalism will ultimately be self-defeating.

Sorry, Marx was a bit more cynical than that. What he truly said was, "A capitalist will sell you the rope he'll hang *you* with." (And then re-write history books so no one knows he did it).

> Nothing is either good nor bad, but greedy
> capitalists make it so.

But I digress. I'm not a communist, but I am extremely cynical about capitalism. Nothing is either good nor bad, but greedy capitalists make it so.

Back on topic. So do you ever notice how many items ring up at the wrong price?

Ever wonder if that at-the-register mark-up is intentional, and not an "honest" mistake. The first clue is it's an error too easily blamed on "careless" employees, "flunkies" doing back-end data entry.

Good rule of thumb for a confidence artist (a.k.a Con man) is: if you're going to trick people, always have an explanation more plausible than the ruse itself.

◇

Consider this case against the mark-up artist. He knows:

1)How many more sales are made when items are marked down. (It's why so many prices are artificially inflated and then the item put on sale). Profit roll in on merchandise purchased at full price. And the real cash cow is how many *more* shoppers are lured in by the mirage of a bargain. A price tag of $6.99 will get more buyers than $8.99. But nothing's stopping that item from writing up at $8.99.

2)The vast percentage of people don't look at their receipt to compare the price charged against the price as marked.

3) Regional franchise managers are rewarded for better sales.

Connecting all the dots, I find it hard to believe the mark-up artist is *not* pulling a fast one.

Be sure to look at your receipts. In some stores, as many as 1 in 5 products ring up at a higher price than marked in certain stores.

We live in a web of ideas, a fabric of our own making.

—*Joseph Chilton Pearce*

Part III

crack

A ~~Jack~~ in the Box

*(A portal of thoughts
that reveal the larger universe)*

The Portal Into a Larger Universe

Joseph Chilton Peirce coined the phrase, " The Crack In The Cosmic Egg" for the title of his first book. He meant that there was a glitch in the fabric of reality ... sort of.

The crack he referred to was a means by which the human mind could escape the bounds of the *quotidian* world we live in and take a step into a larger universe.

He cited "Firewalkers" as examples of how this can be done. These are people who claim they can walk through a pit of blazing hot coals without getting burned.

Science can hardly explain it, although it seems there is some physical evidence that walking softly and slowly across the coals diminishes the fire's ability to burn the skin. Walk softly turns out to be good advice.

Running across, the souls of the feet dig into the coals, and that makes the whole experience much worse.

What if nothing else exists for us simply because we don't accept that anything else can. After all, that's the same premise fire walkers walk on. They don't accept that fire burns. Therefore it doesn't burn them.

But although walking softly may be part of the firewalker's secret, it's a long cry from explaining how they can linger, consumed in fire, for long periods of time and suffer no burns or aftereffects whatsoever.

The explanation they, and Joseph Chilton Peirce, offer, is that it's done with the power of the mind.

It's possible to convince yourself to reject the fact that fire burns.

We all know that fire does burn. But it would seem, if you believe any of this, that consciousness may have some power over it.

The claims of fire walkers or levitating yogis aren't given much credence in Western Thought. We believe the world is based on empirical data, things we can experience directly with our five senses. Western common sense says that since we experience nothing other than what our senses reveal, nothing else exists.

That is a terribly ego-centric world view. You have to admit that even if you don't allow for the possibility of fire walkers or levitating yogis.

The longer I search, the further away the light at the end of reality seems to be.

What if nothing else exists *for us simply* because we don't accept that anything else can. That's the exact same premise fire walkers walk on. They don't accept that fire burns. Therefore it doesn't burn them.

So in our world, yes, imperial data is the supreme driving force—but only because we've chosen to build our world around it.

What we believe are constructs of reality are truly only constructs of our mind. And the mind then constructs civilization around what it believes to be "real," thus making it real by brainwahsing all its citizens into living as though it is real.

I believe the world we see is in fact merely one way to interpret the true, transcendent nature of reality. Our minds, if given free reign, can conceive of and live in something completely other.

We can choose not to participate in reality, just as we can choose not to participate in society.

◇

As you may have noticed, I have been referencing the ideas and philosophies of perhaps half a dozen minds who I consider to be great thinkers—that is, they have contributed to the fabric of human knowledge in some significant way. The best writers and thinkers, I believe, do not come up with their own epiphanies out of thin air.

They manifest from a synthesis of ideas plucked from the ether, or the Akashik records, if you like, that repository of universal knowing.

If the Akashik librarian considers the morsel of your imagination tasty enough, you get a library card and are granted admission into the sprawling labyrinth of thoughts.

Great minds add their own tiny morsel into a single volume of a single encyclopedia sitting on a dusty shelf of one lone bookshelf standing beneath a single arch somewhere within a colossal, vaulted chamber extending further than the mind can imagine.

If the librarian considers the morsel of your imagination tasty enough, you get a library card and are granted admission into the sprawling labyrinth of thoughts.

Our greatest mind are lighthouses guiding us into a larger universe—guideposts towards "The Crack in the Box" of reality where we can break free from the constructs of mind that bind us to this quotidian world of ours.

The longer I search, the further away the light at the end of reality seems to be. But I do believe that together, somehow, we are stumbling towards it.

Original Significance

In a way very similar to how we have mistaken money (a measure of wealth) for wealth itself, we have made the same inverted leap of logic in other areas. Ceremony provides a good example.

Ceremonies, to native peoples, are rites of passage, meaningful events that mark the end of one part of life and the beginning of another. A event to mark transition.

Ceremonies have significant cultural meaning. They knit together the fabric of social structures. The provide meaning, depth, and a sense of shared experiences and purpose. They keep people united. Ceremonies are ties that bind.

But they are not meaningful in and of themselves. Ceremonies mark occasions. They should not be viewed as occasions themselves.

And that's where we've gone off-track.

◇

Why do we wear white?" an initiate asks her Elder.

"It is a symbol of the bright future, a blessing from the sky," the Elder replies.

"And what if I wanted to wear blue?" the novice inquires.

"Why would you want to wear blue?"

"To me," the novice said with conviction, "blue represents the sky, a cloudless future, better than white represents a bright future."

"Then this would be acceptable. This keeps with the intention of the ceremonial significance. The Gods would even applaud, I should think. They will see this as a great honor because it shows that you truly understand our ways, and are not just going through the motions."

But as years turn into centuries and centuries pass through to millennia, some ceremonies degrade into a series of inexplicable eccentricities which the participants can no longer explain in terms of their original significance.

When tradition becomes de coupled from symbolism, the symbol itself becomes the primary method for preserving the tradition.

When the meaning of wearing white is lost and a novice asks, "Why do we wear white?"

The response comes, "This is the way it's always been done."

"And what if I didn't want to wear white?"

"That's silly. Everyone must wear white. It would be sacrilegious not to. The Gods would be offended if you did not! Quit being a blasphemer!"

The ceremonial significance has been lost. Only the ritual remains.

For anyone who wishes to add their own variation to this theme, less and less creative expressions are encouraged, while more and more eccentricities come to overlay the ceremony.

The absence of the connection with original significance, which serves to ground ceremonies to their spiritual meanings, leaves the door open not only to a mis-interpretation of the experience, but to the intentional exploitation of it.

◇

Imagine a ceremony whose initial intent was to connect the supplicants to the Great Spirit. A symbolic aspect of the ceremony—in order to prove the conviction of one's desire to connect with Spirit—may have been to surrender some of one's worldly belongings.

Without remembering of the origin, the initial spiritual intention behind giving up one's possessions may be exploited by the unscrupulous into the notion that initiates must *trade* their most valuable possessions, such as gold, in exchange for the gift of spiritual union.

Conveniently, that gold will be given to the Master of the Ceremony.

As the spiritual element is lost or superseded, the ceremony becomes rooted in the material rather than the spiritual.

The progression may proceed like so:

In a hundred years, not wearing a fancy white dress becomes sacrilege; and the cost of goods which are surrendered becomes negotiable.

A hundred years more, someone may decide to wear a *fancier* white dress with a long, free-flowing train behind it; and someone else may rationalize that it's up to the Master of the Ceremony to decide if the material offering is worthy.

Soon, only the richest and most powerful can afford to partake in the ceremony. The whole tradition now serves to separate people and create a hierarchy, when the original intent was to create unity.

Interpretation and exploitation layer upon each other and meaning is replaced by ritual until the spiritual connection is subverted once and for all, and the idea of ownership, coupled with materialistic pomp and circumstance supersedes all else.

The original spiritual elements become shrouded behind the most elaborate veil of the fanciest white dress.

Mirroring Reality

'll start out with a simple premise: Human researchers are interested in understanding cognition, metacognition and self-awareness. The so-called Mirror test was devised by Darwin as a means to determine if an animal thought its own reflection in a mirror was of indeed themselves or just another animal.

Researches say this test reveals which animals have self-awareness and which do not, but the results have been criticized.

I would criticize the test itself. It proceeds from a false assumption.

The assumption is that the object in the mirror is, in fact, the person or animal being reflected. Humans, of course, believe it is. But in what way? If I look into a mirror, the reflection looks like me … actually it looks like an inverse image of me. But even so, that is where the similarities end.

The reflection does not think, doesn't have self-awareness, isn't alive, or sentient, doesn't talk, breathe, desire, love… I don't believe the reflection is me at all. Does this mean I fail the self-awareness test?

Ever consider asking your reflection in the mirror
if he thinks you're sentient?

Further, I would posit that consciousness itself is merely a mirror … a means of reflecting the external world. I would be more interested to study how and when the person looking into the mirror recognizes self-awareness in other beings.

Why do we claim that humans are self-aware but chimpanzees may or may not be, and that fish certainly aren't? It defies common sense.

Why do humans fail to recognize sentience in animals, but claim to pass the self-awareness test simply by mistaking a reflection in a piece of glass for themselves?

Further, why do we fail to recognize that the Earth itself is alive? That the universe is a living, conscious entity?

Most individuals, and certainly the entire Western Mindset, fail the ultimate Mirror Test—Western humans fail to identify cognition in the majority of life forms reflected in the mirror of their consciousness.

And, failing that, we also fail to identify most of the elements of the universe that are, in fact, alive.

Next time, looking at ourselves in the mirror, we might think to ask our reflection, "Hey reflection, see that being staring at you? Is he sentient?"

On The Existence Of Sentient Organisms Within The Confines Of The Universe

A s a sentient being, I feel qualified to assert that my sentient mind does not feel as though it's living up to its potential. I do not know what a mind's potential is, or truly if there is any limit, or if, after achieving a certain level of consciousness, we would find a big galactic sign saying, "No Thinking Beyond This Point." But one thing I do believe is that too many of us take to heart the over-sized and yet only subliminally visible poster in this life reading, "Thinking is Allowed, but not Encouraged."

You haven't seen this sign? It's the poster hanging on all four walls of every four-walled cubicle we work in, the subliminal context through which televisions are allowed to operate effectively and efficiently and unquestioned by all of us who watch with wide-eyed fascination, with squinting or sleepy eyes. It's the watermark on every diploma we receive, those pieces of paper celebrating how much thinking we've done so far, and glorifying the fact that we have proffered up excessive amounts of money to some institution to translate and qualify that thinking into a numerical unit on a four-point scale.

I don't know quite what it takes for someone to actually live up to their potential, but the best of us, like—picking a name at random—Albert Einstein, don't do so good on that four-point scale. I guess they didn't see the sign.

Cultural Immersion

*D*uring a homestay with a host family—one of the best forms of cultural immersion, the foreigner lives with a native family who, ideally, would only know the native language. Translation isn't possible.

You'd think that would make things harder, that communication would proceed frustratingly slow, like banging your head against a brick wall with the hope of bringing down the wall.

But necessity is the mother of invention, and *learning* a new language from a host family is child's play compared to learning to *translate* a foreign language into your own.

Through translation, we're merely grafting foreign words onto our own language. We're not really learning a new language.

◇

Researchers tell us that children younger than 12 or 13 can more easily learn new languages than adults. Around that age, the brain undergoes its adolescent "demyelination" a physiological process where the mind severs unused neural circuitry. Think of defragmenting your hard drive. However, there is also significant evidence that the brain can always "rewire" itself when it needs to. In other words, those severed neural connections are not lost forever to the deep, dark abysm of mind.

Regardless of how many languages a person can speak, one's First Language always holds a certain special place in determining how your brain thinks, how it processes information.

Cultural beliefs, nuances, stigmas and prejudices are embedded in a language. These are largely "sub-cultural" (like sub conscious), so ingrained in their society's world view that individuals don't even know they have them.

In other words, while language was invented as a means to

express our thoughts, everything from the syntax to the grammar to the overall logic of our First Language plays a huge part in determining how we think.

Learning a new language through cultural immersion recreates, or at least approximates, the experience of learning your First Language, when there was no possibility for translation into anything else (unless baby talk is actually a language).

Cultural beliefs, nuances, stigmas and prejudices
are embedded in a language.

Cultural immersion also does something else: instead of merely learning foreign sounds to represent familiar words, you learn a completely novel way of expressing your thoughts. You learn to think like another tribe. And begin to experience reality as a whole in slightly different ways.

Returning "home" after immersion makes the world you come from seem oddly alien because you begin experiencing it in bizarre new ways.

Most often, the most severe "culture shock" occurs not during an immersion experience, but when returning "home" to place you've never seen before.

When Reality Freezes Over

*W*hen we learn our First Language or any other without translation, we do so by extrapolating (or extracting) the meaning of words from their context. With no linguistic translation for the names of objects like "cup" or "bowl" or "house," our mind has to make the connection itself.

When a parent figure points to a bowl, and says "bowl" enough time, our minds say, "Aha! That's a bowl!"

Once we make that connection, the association is forever after etched in stone, hardens like concrete in our minds. The object and its word become synonymous. When we pigeonhole physical objects into words, arguably, not too much damage is done.

But abstract concepts like "tomorrow," "this," "when," or "wherever" revel just how pivotal language is in determining our reality.

We learn these words through experiential context. No one can point to a "whenever" or a "nowhere."

We learn these through abstract thinking.

When we do, we begin to confuse abstract ideas with tangible words, and pigeonhole, solidify and reduce an otherwise amorphous, fluid reality into the no more than the visible, tangible here and now.

Learning language teaches us that there is no differentiation between *reality* and everyday, quantifiable, classifiable *experience.* Continued learning *through* language reinforces this.

Now that we have grasped the concept of "nowhere," our language now has the right tool in its arsenal to teach us about the concept of "everywhere."

We learned this at a very early age as individuals, and as at a time when our species was very young.

We have "solidified" reality, like freezing water into ice.

◇

Learning a Second Language through translation turns your First Language into a crutch. You learn only to translate the second language into your First. You never truly internalize the second language.

In the same way, learning your First Language becomes a crutch for experiencing reality.

We've been living the adolescence of our species in an "ice age" of reality.

We learn from an early age that language and experience are undifferentiated. If there is no word or concept of something in language, that experience ceases to exist for us. The brain, re-trained at an early age to experience reality through the omnipresent filter of language ceases to be able to experience reality through reality.

It's analogous to how today's cell phones have made us all incapable of remembering anyone's phone number.

Whenever we learn that an intermediary can do our work for us (without any effort from us) what used to seem effortless on our part before the intermediary arrived becomes impossible for us to do on our own, and we come to *need and depend on* the intermediary.

The gene that is believed to give humans the ability for language is not the gene that physically controls our voice box, but the gene that gives us the unique mental ability to transform abstract thoughts into concrete forms, through words, through language.

When this gene popped into the human genome (around 50,000 years ago, geneticists tell us) we began to lose our ability for direct experience of an abstract reality. We started down a road that was destined to lead us into an all-consuming materialist view of our reality.

Ever since, we've been living the past 10,000 of our adolescence as a species in an "ice age" of reality.

The Reality Wave

*S*ome languages have no word for "I." Everything is either "us" or "mine" or "ours." Native speakers have a strong sense of community and little or no sense of themselves as individuals. Many aboriginal languages have no words for nationality; they simply call themselves their word for "People"— like referring to themselves as "Bear" or "Bird."

Therefore, they do not make much distinction between their tribe and another one living down the road. They may have names for those tribes, but the overriding concept is that we are all People first. In the West, we tend to think of ourselves as Americans first and People second.

Native cultures tend to feel less disconnected from their neighbors and focus less on tribal differences. There is less aggression and less warring between tribes whose languages put unity first above division.

Which came first, the culture or the language?

Does the lack of "I" follow a world-view of community, or does a world-view of community prevent the concept of "I" from solidifying into a word. Both are plausible, indeed they both seem to reinforce the other.

So if language orders the mind, and gives logical cohesion to its thoughts, what would our experience of the world be without any language to "solidify" our experiences at all?

How would we experience the world without words to express it? A paradoxical quandary to say the least. Because there'd be no way to express whatever that worldview is.

◇

To borrow a concept from quantum physics,

experience can be thought of as having a wave and particle duality, just like light "waves," and electron "particles."

Electrons travel in a "probability wave" that moves through space like an ocean wave. The act of conscious observation makes it appear as though they exist in a specific place.

Without language and shared experience, an un-filtered experience of the world may exist as reality waves. But our consciousness is so conditioned by shared experiences, that we are bound to experience reality in a particular (particle) way.

Think of the most recognized Gestalt images depicting the duck and the vase in the face. (There are others, like the duck and the rabbit.)

It's possible to conceive of a culture (perhaps alien, if it helps) that has never seen a human face nor a flower vase. To them, these splotches of ink would appear as random as Rorschach inkblot tests.

It's only our shared experiences of faces and vases that forces our minds to interpret patterns into images in the ink. Further, one image will always predominate the other. Your mind may switch between the face and the vase, but will always see the face first, the vase second, and then always back to the first primary image.

Which image is the primary one may actually differ from culture to culture, (whichever is the most common imagery in that culture), which is mostly uniform in all individuals with a shared culture.

Shared, past experiences have a lot to say about how we interpret new experiences.

So what does reality look like in its primary, wavelike form, in the absence of interpretation?

In fact, it seems the more pertinent point is not that language filters interpretation of reality, but filters out more experiences of reality than it lets in.

Every second there are a googols of bits of information (that's 1 with an awful lot of zeroes) flying past our senses. The brain, meanwhile, only has the capacity to convert a small fraction into experience. The remaining bits fly by unnoticed.

Think back to your last experience of driving down the interstate. Remember it? Are you sure?

Driving by that fast, you miss most of the external world. Your world is your car, the thing that's moving with you. You're just along for the ride.

Outside your car, back on solid ground, your consciousness is like your car. You're just along for the ride. You miss most of the external world.

Riding a bike is a good illustration of the point. Imagine riding a bike; you assimilate all the information you can.

Then, afterwords, go walk the same path. You become aware of all the details you overlooked. "Wow, how could I have missed that?" you wonder.

Consciousness experiencing only what it needs to cope with the immediate reality; consciousness is something of a survival mechanism to prevent us from being overwhelmed by it all. In today's crazy fast paced world that evolved overnight, our consciousness has barely had time to adapt. We are constantly overwhelmed, stressed and anxious.

What we choose to see happens subconsciously, informed by all of our experiences up to that point.

We've never seen the world beyond our mind's eye.

Since our past experience of the world plays a huge part in how we experience the world, and as language plays a huge part in how we share our experiences, language becomes one of the factors determining our shared reality.

◇

The psychologist Joseph Pierce postulates that people who walk on fire unscathed do so because they simply have never been taught that they can't.

Philosopher and physicist Amit Gosswami tells us that our ingrained subconscious teachings are impossible to overcome. They are so pervasive in our world view that we don't even realize they exist in our minds at all. We can never truly believe we can fly (and always die when leaping from tall buildings with a single bound) because the subconscious belief that we can't has always been there, ingrained in layers and layers of experience. We've never seen the world beyond our mind's eye.

The conscious mind, Gosswamivsays, can never truly choose, does not actually have fundamental free will because its conception of free will is bound inexplicably to the subconscious prison of our shared experience.

Were it not, any reality we conceived, could in fact, exist.

In fact, the Aborigine people of Australia have very little verbal communication. They believe that verbal communication is so limited that it cannot possibly enable us to express thoughts, but rather, only serves to limit which thoughts can be expressed. In other words: binding experience to an artificial construct (like language) disables the mind's ability to truly experience the exciting, vast sea of realty.

We spend the majority of our days in a frame of mind that's no more than a trance-like state of cultural hypnosis—a waking dream where reality is not visible.

What Animals Think

ince animals don't have language to clog up their consciousness, do they spend their time in a perpetual trance-like state the way Aborigines do?

Many animals sleep the majority of the day. Cats can sleep up to 18 hours or more. Would they do that if there were not some truth or credence to the notion that the dream world is in fact the "real" world as Aboriginal peoples believe?

◇

Do animals have any conception that humans wear clothes or why? (Do humans have really know why we wear clothes, especially those of us who live in tropical environments?)

Ooh! bug bites. Ohh! sunburn. We have developed a sensitivity and aversion to these things precisely because we wear clothes. They are not the reason we started wearing clothes.

But back to animals.

Do cats, dogs, fish, birds, horses or other domesticated animals who share a kinship with a few humans wonder why their person looks different every time they see them?

Do they assume we are like chameleons?

Could it be that chamelions are not in fact camouflaging themselves from predators, but are simply ashamed of the color of their natural skin and sneak into their private *boudoir* to change clothes every time we're not looking?

Cultural Extraction

I t took a few weeks of cultural immersion in the Malagasy culture of Madagascar before I began dreaming in their language. The characters in my dreams were now speaking Malagasy, and I understood perfectly. That's the first sign that you have truly internalized a new language. You begin to dream, to think, in that language.

Peoples who speak only their own native language (not English or any other) view reality differently than we do through our "Western lens." For them, the act of learning English changes their reality in subtle, yet perceptible ways.

So, too, does learning their language,change Western world-views. Our First Language has a very powerful hold on us, yet shifts occur nevertheless.

◇

So what happens then, during the reverse process—not cultural immersion but, cultural extraction?

What happenes after just a week of being immersed in nature, completely separated from cities and technology? They key is-*complete* separation—no cell phone, no laptop, nothing electric). The extreme example would be hunting and gathering off the land, with nothing but clothes on your back (not even that if you lived in a tropical environment.)

I don't have that extreme experience, and my experience only roughly, very roughly, approximates any true cultural extraction. You can try this yourself. Even something as tethered to civilization as primitive camping (don't huddle your tent between RVs) begins to paint the first shades of extraction.

Our culture is so pervasive, so omnipresent, so fast, so addicting that even the humblest form of extricating yourself will start to peel away noticeable layers. It's as if all our cultural experiences are "clogging up the pipes" of our reality. The first drop of liquid drain-o begins to dissolve even some guck.

After just a week in nature, a whole new world emerges. A world that slows considerably. A world of sounds, textures, unfiltered experiences.

Like fasting, the first few days of this de-coupling process are profound experience.

Our prison is most effective. There are no locks, no walls, no bars. Just walls of thought. Invisible until they are not.

I'm writing this after 48 hours. I am thinking, acting, *being* more slowly, more aware of the present. I am beginning to see the forms of animals instead of allowing my mind to categorize them all as "squirrels," "rodents," "insects." As soon as we put a name to them, we pigeonhole them, convinced we know them. I believe this pigeonholing serves to make sure we never do get to know them.

<>

A few days later and the shapes themselves to slip-slide away. I begin thinking formlessly, visualizing amorphous, free-flowing images conjured by wind in trees, calls of nameless beings.

It's an explosion of sensory details. Concepts outshine tangible objects, peacefulness, stillness, replaces hurry and worry. Acceptance of the now circumvents attempts to control an unknowable future by planning.

All of us in culture are locked in specific thought patterns, specific amplitudes and frequency modulations of our brave waves. Experiencing shades of a different kind of reality begins to reveal the invisible walls of a thought prison. This prison is the most effective kind. There are no locks, no walls, no bars. Just walls of thought. Invisible until they are not.

In short, the crucial difference can be summarized in this way: in nature, you learn to focus on the now. In order to cope with civilization, you need to focus on the past and present. Living in the now is ultimately counter-productive.

In nature, you learn to focus on the now. In order to cope with civilization, you need to focus on the past and present. Living in the now is ultimately counter-productive.

Our reality there consists of past and future abstractions. We focus on artificial time-tables, prepare reports about how future quarterly reports compare to previous quarterly reports. We create spreadsheets.

Commuting to work, your mind conceives of the projects you'll do that day, events that unfolded yesterday, how they will ripple into tomorrow. You focus on the cars around you, playing a game of chess, trying to anticipate your next move and theirs, trying to merge lanes without getting pulverized.

These things are all irrelevant to living your life. In fact, these things prevent living. Yet these are the things we need to focus on in order to survive the world we've imposed on ourselves, grafted onto a natural, forgotten way of life.

What do I mean they're irrelevant? you might ask. They are very relevant. They put food on the table.

I can't argue. Yet they are meaningless in and of themselves. You can't eat a quarterly statement. Quarterly reports and projections have no objective reality. Only a subjective one.

Even a dollar bill has greater "meaning" than a spreadsheet. At least it has an objective reality. Objectively, it's a piece of paper with green ink. It takes on a subjective reality of the value of $1 because, collectively, we agree it does. A dollar does have a an objective reality, albeit a useless one. It may be green, but you can't eat it.

Now look at your spreadsheet. It presents piles and piles of information that is useful to us only because we agree that it's useful. That's the extent of its reality. Purely subjective.

But civilization trains our minds into confusing subjective reality with objective reality. You are so brainwashed that you believe that the things your mind is trained to focus on, to think of as important, are "real."

All the data in a spreadsheet is completely theoretical. It is devoid of objective reality. It exist without even being printed on a piece of paper. Where it exists in a circuit board, it's no more than a random series of electrical impulses, which a computer interprets into a seemingly ordered series of 1s and 0s, which you then need a piece of software (running another binary sequence) to interpret into patterns of light which your eyes interpret into a language which our minds have been trained to confuse with reality.

Worried About Being Worried

Of course you may be inclined to argue that living in the primordial forest, with all your awareness of the "present" and all that, your life cannot truly be worry-free or without a concept of the future.

What about worrying about where your next meal will come from, or whether it's going to eat you instead of you eating it?

Aborigines are aware of the need to eat in the future as well as the possibility of themselves being eaten, and getting sick, and dying. Of course they are. And I don't mean to suggest their lives are absolutely idyllic. And I don't advocate that we all abandon civilization and return to the primordial ooze. But we can and should abandon some aspects of civilization and some technologies. Some are as harmful as others are useful.

If you truly lived every moment in the present, you would realize there's no need to worry about where your next meal is going to come from. You'd be aware you need to eat, but not that you'd need to eat in the future. You'd think, "I always need to eat." It's a subtle but important shift in world-view.

Besides, nature is the literal Garden of Eatin'. There's no lack of food or variety. As long as we keep our population in check, there's always a bounty of food. Only after we started growing our own food did we have to start worrying, what if there isn't enough for everybody? Farming allowed our population to explode beyond any reasonable level the natural environment could sustain.

In almost all populations, nature has ways of limiting populations. There's evidence that females of all different species become inexplicably infertile when populations reach a terminal threshold. Predation (predators eating you) also keeps things in check.

Yet, as a human living in the jungle, you wouldn't really worry too much about predators eating you. You feel fear, that's an emotion. You'd probably feel all emotions more keenly than we do today, so dulled by overestimation and numbed with Prozac.

But today we spend more hours thinking about making time to go to the grocery store, or what we're going to cook for dinner than 100,000 generations of humans ever spent worrying about what (or who) was for dinner.

We ate what was available (sometimes we were), and were never slaves to the idea that we had any say in the matter.

It is today's mind set (an illusion) that we are in control which turns us into perpetual worry warts, fixated on the thought that we will lose control.

Today we spend so much time worrying about life that we fail to live it.

(You can't lose something you never had.)

Then we worry that we're going to lose our lives to death.

(You can't lose something you never had.)

Besides, it's only our myopic outlook, limited to the physical world, that paints the ridiculous notion that our death is the end *of everything*. It's merely a transition. Cultures all over the world realized and accepted this for thousands of years. They were aware of it, not worried about it, or in dread of it.

They lived in the now.

Living in nature, you realize that control is as much of an illusion, without objective reality, without meaning outside your own mind, as an earnings statement.

The Way We Were

efore the rise of cities, some evidence shows the average person's life-span was greater than 70 years, a longevity milestone urban civilizations are only now beginning to eclipse with the help of Western Medicine practiced in the First World. In other words, it took us 6,000-8,000 years of trial-and-urban-error to regain the lifespan hunter-gathers lived on the plains.

There is also evidence that humans lived to ripe old ages and were much less "petrified" than our elders today. Less wrinkled skin, less diseases, less male pattern-baldness.

Why? Less toxins in the atmosphere, no pollution, ozone holes, BPA, high-fructose corn syrup, organic produce, the list goes on and on.

And on.

And on.

And on.

It all adds up to less degeneration of the telomere (the ends of DNA which cause aging), less (and possibly no) cancer, less heart disease, better health and longevity, and the list goes on and on.

And on.

And on.

And on..

So where, then, does the myth that the "average" age of pre-agricultural people lived only to be 20 or 30 years old come from?

Absurdly, the myth comes from archeologists meshing together all the deaths from old age (60s, 70s, even 80s) with an enormous number of infant mortalities, and deaths from natural causes (such as being eaten by dinner, instead of the other way round).

The number of unnatural early deaths far outnumber the people who actually lived to old age. But those who did lived to ripe old ages.

The associated error in logical thinking is that the hunter-gather lifestyle was inherently dangerous and that there was a daily threat of being eaten by ravenous lions or other predators. That, too, is non-sense.

Carnivores are at the top of the food chain. Omnivores up even higher.

Very few animals seemed to have preyed upon humans, unless there really was no other choice. They would kill in self-defense, but only kill us for dinner in extreme cases.

In the majority of cases, the evidence tells us, this appears to happen only when, say, a lion and a human were competing for the same dinner. Or if we had the misfortune of wandering into a lion's territorial domain or their cubs felt threatened by us. Or perhaps when a myopic hunter mistook a lion for a mammoth. (Common mistake, I'm told, before the invention of glasses).

No predator seems to have had a preference for human flesh.

Even in the 21st century we see evidence that carnivores tend not to eat other carnivores, but rather eat (almost exclusively) vegetarian animals, such as cows and chickens. Humans do not tend to eat lions or gazelles, just as lions or gazelles tend to not eat humans.

Dying during a hunt would have been considered noble, while living to old age likely would have implied a sense of cowardice (based on what we think we know about stone-aged hunters.)

If not everything we know is wrong, many males (who were hunters) would have tended to prefer being killed by wild beasts than live to be 70.

Fossils of women and children are rarely found to have been eaten. However, a larger number of women died in childbirth, bringing that erroneous "average age" down further still.

All of this led myopic archeologists to the contention that before the invention of the proverbial "guns, germs, steel" and civilization, human predation was omnipresent, and hunter-gathers lived short, stress-filled lives that make today's office jobs look idyllic and like a "return to the Garden."

But all things being equal, lions and other predators were not the ones who aggressively stalked humans. Any humans that suffered their deaths at the hands of wild beasts seemed to have had it coming.

Others lived to ripe old ages and, could petrified fossils talk, no doubt tell us, "We were living rich, full lives to ripe old ages while your grandparents were still in diapers!"

Mind out of Time

I sit for long hours at a time. Sometimes listening to soul-stirring music. Sometimes thinking thoughts. Sometimes absorbed by visions. I think of it as the Act of Being. No, no *act*, no action. Just Being.

Momentary moments of silence change tracks for the train of thought. Thoughts shift and ideas change and sometimes the last ones are forgotten as they are built upon, and the surface level is lost for the depths. Sometimes it's the same song over and over, again and again. A song or a thought caught in an endless dance with your mind.

Let, on the inhale.

Go, on the exhale.

Surrender to swimming in an ocean of emotion, being, thoughtless, formless, senseless. Then let your mind run free in the afterimage, the vision of emotion. But not with the thoughts, just with the memory.

Moments of perfect and pure being—moments with mind so thoughtless, moments cease to exist and only their substance remains.

Relax, on the inhale.

Accept, on the exhale.

Like canvas, oils and frame dematerializing and only the image remaining.

There's a measurable gap in the firing of the neurons that create thoughts. They say our mind is always processing reality some fraction of a second after it occurs. So what we perceive as the present, is truly the past.

Time slows in moments of great trauma.

An experience of reality in slow motion. Mind-time.

Being is mind out of time. Being wedging itself between

thoughts like a cat cozying up under a soft blanket in front of firelight. Being sinks into the space between mind and time, wedges into the space between perception and action. The ultimate freedom from the prison.

No judgments, no action, no reaction, no thinking, no time, no place.

This might be known as meditation. But there is no knowing. This is Being.

What if we choose to eradicate ourselves from this Earth,
by whatever means?
The Earth goes nowhere.
And in time, it will regenerate, and all the lakes will be pristine.
The rivers, the waters, the mountains, everything will be green again.
It'll be peaceful.
And you know why?
Because the Earth has all the time in the world and we don't.

— *Oren Lyons*

All follow deep in trance
Lost in a catatonic dance
Know no future
Damn the past
Blind, warm, ecstatic
Safe at last...

— *Natalie Merchant*

Part IV

Remember How It All Began:
The ~~Apple~~ And The ~~Fall~~ Of Man
    ice age   *rise*

The Garden of Evolution

I don't believe in evolution.

But perhaps that needs some explanation. I believe evolution is vastly misunderstood, and I don't ascribe to the misconception of evolution. So perhaps it would be more accurate to say that it's not evolution that I don't believe in, but rather the method by which we believe evolution works: natural selection.

Survival of the Fittest. Hogwash.

The theory takes as its premise the notion all of life is in competition with all other life forms on the planet—including members of one's own species. Males are perpetually at war with other males for the "right" to the fittest female. Females are perpetually one-up-ing each other for access to the best male genes in order to endow their offspring with superior fittest-ness.

Survival of the fittest also presupposes that all mutations are random errors in DNA replication, mostly harmful, only a handful ever serving any beneficial purpose. The individuals who just happen to be successful mutants survive while others die out. Rubbish.

Both of these premises (randomness and competition) by which Natural Selection supposedly operates evolution are fatally flawed. These two notions, however, were very much in line with the flood Western thought during Darwin's lifetime and directed, indeed bound, his thinking about the subject.

In brief, the general belief at the time (the infancy of the Industrial Revolution and the rejection of the supreme Church) almost demanded those two premises. Western minds, free at last from 1,000 years of bondage by Catholic dogma were intent on finding alternative hypotheses for how the world worked. From dogma to stigma, the West rejected the existence of God, anything even remotely spiritual, and embraced the Western scientific method. Through the proper understanding and application of science and industry, nothing was beyond the comprehension of man.

Ironically, Church-going was still all the rage. Religious practices were required; atheism was taboo. Yet it was the oppression of the Church that had made people turn away from God. Keeping up appearances by being a devout Catholic was never even a question.

Science grew out of the rejection of religion. That explains why today, those two notions are thought to be as contradictory as classical physics and quantum physics.

An *a-priori* notion is something believed to be
a sovereign truth, not open to question.
We have a lot of them. Mostly wrong.

Yet like the two physics, the resolution of paradox between science and spiritual beliefs must be found before we can ever hope to find a complete theory of everything.

◇

A belief is a dangerous thing. Cultural ignorance of its own underlying beliefs is terrifying. (Such as how science evolved as a mutation of religion and the Survival of the Fittest ideologies.)

Ignorance of the rational behind irrational beliefs allows those beliefs to be almost impervious to deeper examination. Because the underlying belief is invisible, it is erroneously believed to be *a-priori*.

An *a-priori* notion is something believed to be a sovereign truth, not open to question, an underlying foundation of logic and above the law of the scientific method.

False a-priories are mirages of mind, just like a mirage in a desert.

A man dying of thirst who sees a mirage will not question the existence of water, until perhaps, he chokes while drinking sand. Drinking sand is clearly an irrational behavior as any objective observer would see. But dying of thirst, the mind needs the vision to be real and doesn't question it. It is a false a-priori belief.

In individuals, Sarte would call these omnipresent, invisible beliefs the "ah-ha principle."

Through psychoanalysis, Sarte reasoned that these beliefs could be rooted out by the psychiatrist (never by the patient), and when the patient was told of them, he would jump out of his chair and exclaim, "Ah-ha! That's the reason I act the way I do!"

Sarte also proposed that there was a "collective unconscious" to our entire culture.

I postulate that the "ah-ha" principle of humanity that arose in the 19th century was: "We reject god; but we must go to Church in case he's real (its cheap insurance). But understanding the world as random and competitive allows us to explain everything without need for the God hypothesis."

Science as we know it today offers us our best guesses about how seemingly inexplicable phenomena can be explained. In the 19th century, when modern science was just getting started, there were many unexplained phenomena in the world.

Ignorance of the rational behind irrational beliefs
allows those beliefs to be all but impervious
to deeper examination.

So although the world was not understood, the intellectual elite were bound and determined to explain away God. No short order.

The explanation they came up with came from the synthesis of other cultural obsessions of the time: Building bigger, better, larger, more powerful industrial machines (otherwise known as the Industrial Revolution) and in so building them, amass enormous collections of more and more money, prestige, power.

Without God, the universe was seen as random, unpredictable, and only our newest, latest, greatest biggest machines could tame nature. Technology might never explain the Universe, but it could certainly subdue it. It was a matter of life and death. Humanity saw itself at war with the ravaging forces of nature.

Amassing fortunes and empires by re-making the world in their own image, successful industrial capitalists took it as gospel that they should feel no guilt for achieving financial success and rising through the ranks of society by stepping on the backs of everyone in their way. How did they skirt the inherent moral dilemmas, get around even considering the human cost of their ruthless empire-building? Simply put, they believed that they were successful because they were smarter, savvier, more cutthroat than other, less successful capitalists. It was a capitalist-eat-capitalist world. It was triumph or fall on your face. Empire building was a competition against nature and against the other capitalists.

> Ironically, "Survival of the fittest" was coined not by Darwin, but by Herbert Spencer, an economist.

And out of all of this came a brilliant and inescapable synthesis. Thus followed the notion that everything, all of life, was in a desperate competition for survival. Winner take all. Survival of the fittest. It was a notion that spoke to successful Capitalists and floundering ones all the same. It reinforced the successful ones' amoral nonchalance about the human cost of their success just as it gave floundering members of lower classes something to hope for. Life was a competition, and it could be won by anyone, as long as they didn't care about the price of victory. Through cutthroat competition, the strong could survive.

Survival of the fittest was a notion perfectly in-line with the cultural mind set of the time..

In an ironic twist on the evolution of the idea of evolution, it was not in fact Darwin himself who ironed out the modern-day "understanding" of natural selection. It was Herbert Spencer, an economist, who drew parallels between his own economic theories and Darwin's biological ones. "Survival of the fittest" was Spenser's phrase.

I the fifth edition of On the Origin of Species, Dawrin adopted it, and the modern day understanding of Evolution made its way into our textbooks.

Survival of the fittest was an idea created in its own image. Born in a hall of mirrors if you will of self-reinforcing beliefs.

It is a brilliantly articulated theory that perfectly illucidates the cultural ah-ha principle of the time yet does nothing to explain evolution. In fact, it is probably the very antithesis of the way evolution really comes about.

The Bonsai Tree of Life

*T*he *universe is* not a hostile place. Not a place of competition and not a random, disordered, frightening place. Nature thrives on cooperation instead. The natural world is a circle of life that completes itself, not competes with itself. The circle forms a whole where everything is linked inexplicably together. The view that nature is a competition where only the strong survive is absolute rubbish.

As such, evolution is a dance, a multitude of species working together to evolve alongside one another, for mutual benefit. Individuals within a species change fluidly, in response to each other, their environment and the tree of life.

It's like a flock of birds migrating. The flock changes direction all together, in one fluid motion, each individual responding to the subtle movements of the birds around it. There is no first bird to alter course; there is no last. The flight-path simply *evolves*.

◇

I would like to turn our attention now to bonsai trees.

If you ask a bonsai enthusiast how they keep their trees so small, they might be apt to reply, "I don't keep my trees small. They do it themselves."

The art of bonsai, in essence, is to alter the tree's natural environment so much to convince the tree that it can make a better living as a small tree than as a large one.

Now this is not a random mutation, nor is it adverse. This is evidence that the tree is cooperating with its environment through spontaneous changes at an individual level. We're not talking about trees just being shorter; we're talking about miniature leaves; miniature pinecones.

Mutations are not by chance, some just so happening to be beneficial as Darwinian evolutionists believe . Species are not locked in an endless "struggle for survival" in a chaotic, unpredictable environment working against them. What an absurd notion.

The bonsai tree is a metaphor for evolution: it is not a conflict with nature, but a cooperation. There is an interdependency between all living things (the environment is alive, too). As one changes, so does the other.

A dance; not a war.

Civilization in a Bubble

*I*f *ancient lost* civilizations were around today, looking at the way we interpreted their creation myths, they'd likely be rolling in their long-lost tombs.

One of the oldest still-practiced religions on Earth is Zoroastrianism. We believe it arose based on the teachings of Zoroaster who may have lived around 600 BCE.

Yet there are some interpretations of their creation myths and traditions which would make the religion much more ancient, originating as long ago as 18,000 BCE—twenty thousand years ago.

The Zoroasters tell stories about Gods battling in the sky. The great battles they tell us triggered terrible winters that lasted for generations here on earth. One of the two sky gods led the Zoroastrians deep underground to take refuge. (This parallels the Flood story, but this story describes more of a long ice age than a flood).

> 18,000 years is plenty of time for civilization to evolve from simple towns and villages into technological super-powers. Twice.

Some scholars suggest that these stories—the flood and the Zoroastrian cataclysm—are related. The Zoroastrian cataclysm being the beginning of the last ice age, and the great flood being the worldwide result of the last ice age's thawing when melting ice caps flooded the land.

Note that during an ice age, the whole world isn't under ice... just an awful lot of it. The proverbial Garden of Eden is not precluded from existing. In fact, modern interpretations of its geographic location places it in an idyllic climate for a pocket of humans to thrive during the last ice-age. Then, of course, the Garden of Eden flooded when the ice caps melted. And today lies off shore in the

Persian Gulf, where ancient riverbeds reveal that the three rivers mentioned in the fable converge.

The last ice age verified by geologists began 18,000 years ago and ended 10,000 years ago.

The proverbial quest for a needle in a haystack would be child-play compared to the incomprehensibly vast search for a lost civilization in rock strata.

The more creation myths I read, the more and more clear it seems to me that humanity's history is inexorably tied with these two key geological events, and that we do in fact have some kind of forgotten history between (and potentially even before) this time.

Any history that we did have prior to global glaciation 18,000 years ago and the ensuing great flood/thaw 10,000 years ago would certainly be all but completely lost to the geological record. Just imagine how long 10,000 years is.

It is longer ago than all of recorded history.

Now imagine how long 18,000 years is.

It is longer than two incarnations of all of recorded history.

18,000 years is plenty of time for civilization to evolve from simple towns and villages into technological super-powers. Twice.

◇

Do you think your computer, your home, your cell phone, books, even stainless steel skyscrapers, can survive 2 cataclysmic global events and 20,000 years or erosion?

About the only thing that will survive will be solid structures build from stone (think the sphinx) or anything deep enough underground.

In fact there is a great underground city called Derinkuyu in Turkey that archeologists know to have been home to over 30,000 people, livestock, and there is even evidence for subterranean farms.

Native American Indian tribes, too, have stories of living with the "snake people" in deep underground labyrinths, and their creation story has them rising up out of the ground to begin civilization "again." Their stories hold that civilization existed before and was wiped out.

As a civilization, we have a very, myopic definition of history.

According to historians, dinosaurs vanished about 65 million years ago ... and then not much happened until the rise of Western Civilization about 8,000 years ago.

Started, or started over?

In the vast geologic record, where millions of years are compressed into 2 feet of stratified rock, it is fairly easy (and understandable) to lose say, 10,000 – 20,000 years here and there. It seems like it would be indefatigably hard to find those missing millennia, especially when the geological record is sending floods and iceages your way to deter your efforts.

The proverbial quest for a needle in a haystack would be childplay compared to the incomprehensibly vast search for a civilization in rock strata.

And meanwhile all we're left with is ambiguous creation myths that could mean anything.

If another ice age and flood pairing happen on Earth today, is seems likely that, 20,000 years from now, our own digital civilization will be merely a streak of soot buried within miles of stratified rock.

Air bubbles in rock can sometimes give lucky geologists clues into the atmosphere on earth at any given time. Perhaps when the geologists of the future are digging in rocks, they will discover evidence of our civilization in a bubble.

"Well, we know that just before the last ice age," geologists of the future will say, "There was an unprecedented increase in the levels of CO_2 and Methane in the air. We have no idea what caused that at a time in Earth's history long before the rise of human civilization."

A Flood of Stories

*T*here *are* *literally* hundreds of independent myths that reference the Great Flood, scattered across all six of today's inhabited continents.

A vast majority of these flood stories play a part not only in cultural mythologies but a central role in creation stories. The best known example in the Western Tradition is the Bible. Noah's flood is arguably the first historically verifiable event in the Old Testament. Biblical characters were living to the ripe old age of 900 before Noah came round.

The Noah figure also appears in the *Epic of Gilgamesh*, which pre-dates the Bible, and is the earliest known written text. Noah, who goes by the name Utnapishtim, was told the build an Ark by God.

It's much the same everywhere.

A flood story is the first historically verifiable event in mythologies around the world. More over, the flood is the creation myth of an indefinably large number of unconnected cultures.

The parallels between the Flood story in its hundreds of various incarnations are mind-boggling. The Gods (a monotheistic God in the Hebrew tradition is the exception) decided to destroy mankind and start over. An afternoon in the public library can unearth at least 70 variations of this myth.

As stunning as the sheer number of variations is, the wide geographic separation of these myths is even more astounding. Africa, Asia, North and South America, all share the same story.

Seems odd that this same one story was the oldest story ever recorded in so many cultures, doesn't it? It seems unlikely that the knowledge of writing arose so uniformly across the world.

Are we to believe that the knowledge of writing simply spontaneously emerged all round the world after the waters receded?

It seems equally as odd that the same story was "imagined" by so many cultures independently.

Taking into account both these apparent paradoxes, one conclusion presents itself.

It seems more likely that the knowledge of writing had been pre-existent, only all the stories written down *before the flood* were lost *in the flood.*

An afternoon in the public library can unearth
at least 70 variations of this myth.

And since the myth is so widespread, it follows that the flood must have been global.

The story of the flood, therefore, is the first written history from so many cultures not because this truly was the creation of the world, but rather that it is the first story to survive after the flood ubiquitously devastated all cultures previously thriving on Earth.

What could have caused such a widespread flood? Turn the page?

When Earth Freezes Over

*A*ccording to mainstream archeologists who hold that civilization began about 8,000-10,000 years ago, the Great Flood is merely a biblical myth.

But geologists know that the end of the last ice age was 8,000-10,000 years ago.

Anthropolgists are also at a head-scratching loss to explain the inexplicable rise of agriculture 8,000 years ago. It's as if humanity just took a quantum leap forward, they say. The archeological holds reveal evidence for hunter-gather tribes living about 18,000-20,000 years ago, then that record is strangely silent until agriculture's spontaneous rise about 12,000 years later.

Well, first off think about those time lines. What's the first thing that jumps out at you? To me, it's their lack of precision. It's kind of, maybe, give or take 2,000 years or so.

In geological time, 2,000 passes is the blink of an eye, and I can easily see how we can't precisely place the year of the great flood. I couldn't expect any anthropologist to say, "Eureka! The Great Flood occurred on August 15th, 18,167 B.C. at 1:57 in the afternoon!"

Be that as it may, a 2,000 year window—microscopic in Earth-time—is colossal in human-time. Just look at known civilization's meteoric rise over the past 2,000 years—from bows and arrows to computers.

Seems to me we have some pretty conspicuously convergent time lines:

- The end of the last ice age (causing the Great Flood)
- When recorded civilization began
- The Christian Bible's belief that the Earth itself is 6,000 years old (again 2,000 years is nothing),
- The inexplicable quantum leap of agriculture.

- The conspicuous silence of the geological record from about 18,000-10,000 years ago.

We think of all of these things as happening long ago.

But they happened relative recently in history as measured by any other yardstick than that of human civilization.

Further, all those distant events didn't happen at different times in the past; they all happened around precisely *the same time.*

In school, we might learn about the Flood in religion class. We might learn about agriculture in History class. We might learn about the invention of writing in English class.

In geological time, 2,000 passes in the blink of an eye

We learn about each of these events separately, and we don't connect the dots.

But the timeline is self-evident. These events converged at one moment in history.

And what deduction can we draw from that hypothesis? .

◇

Advanced civilizations were wiped out by the Great Flood. There are a number of technologies which all seem to have been spontaneously invented when the waters of the flood reseeded.

- Agriculture
- Writing
- Complex Cities
- Indoor plumbing,
- Megalithic stone structures

There is no evidence for the development of any of this. It's as if humanity just snapped a finger and there they were.

But none of this could have developed overnight.

All this technology must have been invented during the 10,000 years lost to the geological record (washed away in the flood.)

Today we scratch our heads wondering how the Egyptians build the pyramids.

The largest, at Giza, consists of 2.3 million blocks, each weighting up to 80 tones! Some of those blocks were transported from over 500 miles away! What!?

We've tried to duplicate that today, and haven't succeeded even with modern equipment.

Yet we're expected to believe Egyptians did it without the wheel, without engineering schematics, without machinery.

The contention held by archeologists that the Great Pyramid was built in 2,560 BC by the Egyptians as a tomb for Pharaoh Khufu over a mere 20-year period seems patently absurd.

The evidence for it is dreadfully thin, too. About the best evidence they have is circumstantial and it's this: The Egyptian civilization occupied the same place as the Pyramids.

The "Egyptian" Sphynx, too, is equally misunderstood. Here's an interesting anecdote about that particularly large megalith: even mainstream meteorologists agree that the type of erosion seen on the Sphynx is typical of monsoons, not desert wind and sand.

It makes more sense that an advanced pyramid- and Sphinx-building civilization arose in a tropical rainforest ideal for life (like the Maya) than in an inhospitable, arid desert.

We know for certain that the Sahara desert is located at a unique place on the globe where climate shifts are cyclical and dramatic. You might have a hard time wrapping your mind around this one, but this notion is the least contentious, the most accepted by every discipline of mainstream science.

About 18,000-20,000 years ago, the Sahara was a rainforest, at the same time that the Earth was experiencing its last Glacial Maximum (the peak of an ice age.)

It's as if Earth itself experiences a change of season every 20,000 years. From wet to dry, from cold to warm.

It's a common misconception that during an ice age the whole world is covered in ice and snow. Not so. During an ice age, there are significantly larger polar regions, with more of Earth's water locked up in glaciers. 20,000 years ago, the ice sheet on Earth's northern polar region covered Europe to the Meditaranean and North America to the Great Lakes. But Earth's equatorial region was tropical.

The time line for when a pre-flood civilization would have thrived matches the erosion evidenced on the Sphynx. And it makes more sense that an advanced pyramid- and Sphinx-building civilization arose in a tropical rainforest ideal for life on planet Earth (like the Maya) than in an in-   hospitable, arid desert.

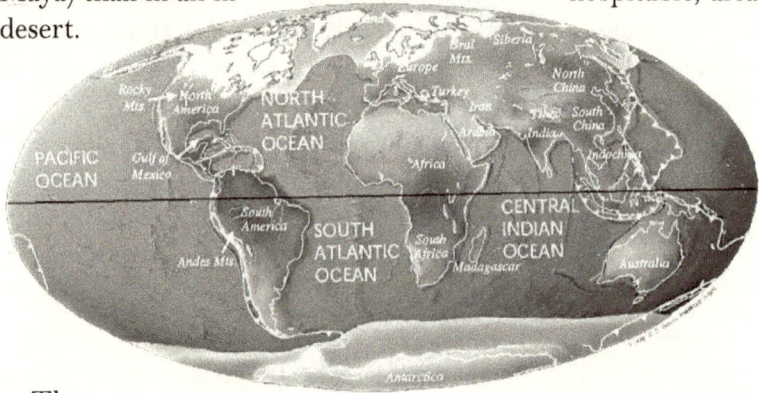

The   convergence of all this evidence is   mind-boggling, and, in my opinion, makes common sense.

Another megalithic construction project, the great heads on Easter Island, are also inexplicable to modern scholars. More mysterious than why they were built, is the mystery of how an isolated people on a small island could have accomplished this feat.

Easter Island today is scarcely big enough to even have that much stone, let alone support a large enough human population to quarry it.

Today, rising sea levels caused by global warming threaten our entire planet. One of the areas that will flood first is the low-lying islands in Oceania (Easter island, Polynesia, etc).

There is a lot of land beneath the relatively shallow seas in Oceania. In fact, the entire Indian Ocean, which spans the region between the Indian Subcontinent and Australia, is the shallowest

ocean in the world. Its deepest point is only 7,000 feet. The other
major oceans of the world, the Pacific and the Atlantic, are each
about 28,000 feet deep.

Remember that an ice age means significantly more ice, which
floats above the surface, traps water, and therefore lowers sea
levels substantially. During the last glacial maximum, sea level
was approximately 7,000 feet lower than it was today.

And that would have meant the area now beneath the 7,000
foot Indian Ocean would have been dry land. The Indian Subcontinent would have extended south and Australia would have
been connected to Asia.

This civilization could have thrived for perhaps as long as
10,000 years (a time when the archeological record is silent.)

20,000 years ago, Easter Island was not an isolated island at
all. It was smack dab in the middle of a huge continent about
200,000-300,000 square miles large during the precise period
when the geological record is conspicuously silent, during the
time before the Great Flood.

In my humble opinion, it is undeniable that an advanced, global
human civilization was thriving on Earth 20,000 ago, and was
completely wiped out by the Great Flood.

This civilization could have thrived for perhaps as long as
10,000 years (a time when the archeological record is silent.)

Well, not completely silent. As the Zen koan illumines, "Silence
is spoken here." It's a silence that speaks volumes.

What are the Egyptian pyramids and their twins, the Mayan
pyramids, half-way across the world, trying to tell us?

What do the heads at Easter Island say?

If it's impossible that known civilizations built these things, it
must be the case that civilizations unknown to us did.

It makes perfect sense that when a great flood swept over the
land, the only things to survive were made of solid rock. Geologists and climatologists tell us the last ice age ended suddenly,

perhaps as little as 1-2 years. So any civilizations around at that time wouldn't have had very much time to prepare.

What are the Egyptian pyramids and their twins, the Mayan pyramids, half-way across the world, trying to tell us? What do the heads at Easter Island say?

Probably the best they could do was hop in a couple arks and save their own lives. Those lucky enough to buy passage on the big boats would be doomed to watch in horror as their entire civilization, all their technology, was lost below the waves.

For the sake of argument, let's say it's all true. A Great Flood destroyed civilization when the last ice age suddenly ended.

What might cause a whole ice age to suddenly end?

What the heck caused the Great Flood?

It likely was something that caused a tremendous surge in sea levels initially, as well as a long-term rise. The initial surge would have wiped out civilization in one fell swoop and eradicated any evidence that it had ever existed. The long-term rise would have ensured all evidence remained entombed.

A meteor impact or a reversal of the magnetic polls are two likely possibilities. But there is another...

Mass Extinction!

*"I don't think that many people have actually looked into the idea
that some natural catastrophe caused civilizations to disappear. How
many of them might have disappeared that we don't even know
about, maybe because it happened 20 thousand or 30 thousand years
ago? What we are focused on now is civilization of the past five
thousand years. Chinese history and Egyptian history is about all we
go back to."*

—U.S. Congressman Dana Rohrabacher , 2011

A lmost everyone has heard of the extinction of the dinosaurs 65 million years ago. But there have in fact been major global extinction events occurring for millions of years on Earth—in fact since the very beginning of life. In fact, the Cretaceous–Tertiary extinction event, which wiped out the dinosaurs was the most recent of the five major extinction events in Earth's history which all occurred hundreds of millions of years ago.

In addition to five major extinction events in Earth's geological history, there are 15 lesser extinctions the fossil record speaks of.

That's 20 known global events in all, believed to have been caused either by meteor impacts or dramatic climate changes on Earth. The solar system is replete with meteors, and hundreds of millions of years ago, fossil evidence suggests they were impacting the Earth much more frequently. Within the last 100 million years or so, our solar system—and Earth itself—seem both to have settled down somewhat.

The anomaly in the time line is the most recent—and relatively smaller—extinction event in Earth's history which occurred just 50,000 years ago.

No one knows exactly why it occurred, simply that it did. There are a few front-running theories as to what might have happened. One of the most widely accepted attributes it to human activity.

Wait, that's an accepted theory among scientists? you ask. Are we talking pseudoscience here?

No, not yet.

Even according to "accredited" scientists, humans are believed to have been hunting species to extinction for perhaps as long as 300,000 years.

As human activity reaches a crescendo, the estimated extinction rate is 68 species every day, 5,000% higher than normal.

50,000 years ago, we over hunted enough that we brought the Earth to its first major human-incited tipping point where the entire food chain broke down. A domino effect of extinction occurred at a rate that far outpaced the "background" extinction rate, which is believed to be about 1-10 species per year, on average.

Any of this sounding familiar?

With deforestation and global warming and other human activity reaching a crescendo, the estimated number of species dying out today is about 5,000% higher than the background extinction rate, or about 25,000 species per year, on average. (That's 68 species every day!)

Some scientists have called what we're experiencing today the "sixth great extinction."

And it's probably not the first time we're the ones to blame.

◇

The official name for human-based extinction events is "second-order predation." Ominous sounding somehow, isn't it?

Why second-order? Well, think of it like two-degrees of separation. Although our activities like pumping CO_2 and methane into the air today at unprecedented rates is killing 68 species per day, eventually, a tipping point will be reached that topples the *entire* food chain.

That's exactly what many mainstream scientists believe human activity caused 50,000 years ago.

Now, those same mainstream scientists see these ancient humans as stone-age hunter gatherers using stone knives and wearing bear skins.

But how much damage can a few scattered nomadic groups wielding spears really do?

I suppose if we believe the Egyptians built the pyramids without the use of the wheel or engineering schematics or heavy machinery, it make sense that stone-age hunters caused a great extinction event with their spears.

Humans and climate change are both implicated
in causing a global extinction event 50,000 years ago.

But whose to say that this man-made extinction event 50,000 years ago wasn't caused by a previous incarnation of human civilization? By an advanced civilization's successful bid at destroying itself?

It could have happened.

Heck, it could have happened during the Cuban Missile Crisis in 1961. And then neither you nor I would be here considering these ideas.

Instead, our progeny, born 50,000 years from now would be having this conversation about how Earth's sixth great extinction event was caused by stone-aged cave men hunting with spears.

◇

Back to the science for a moment.

Another theory for the last great extinction event that does not blame humanity is severe climate change. There is a known major climate change that coincides in the geological calendar with the last extinction event 50,000 years ago.

But why was there a massive climate change? Scientists fall back on the old standby, "meteor or comet impact" theory.

Possible. Sure.

But we don't know for certain what caused the climate change.

We simply know it happened, and that it likely contributed to the extinction event, an event whose ultimate cause we also don't know for certain.

There's some evidence to support the meteor impact theory, such as nanocrystals in the ancient ice, the kind that form in the presence of extreme temperatures that would accompany a meteoric impact.

> Our modern cultural beliefs and prejudices
> support as much conjecture as truth.

Here's what we do know:

1. Anatomically modern humans walked the Earth 50,000 years ago (up to 300,000 years ago).

2. The climate changed drastically 50,000 ago (it got colder -- ice age cold).

3. A worldwide extinction event occurred, which the human species survived.

4. Human activity produced a "tipping point."

5. There is evidence of nanocrystals in the soil, evidencing a release of extreme heat which is also associated with the tipping point.

I find it interesting that both humans and climate change are both implicated in causing a global extinction event 50,000 years ago. No, it's more than interesting. More than a coincidence. It's suspicious. Is it such a stretch to connect the dots here?

◇

Aside from a meteor hit, what else could explain all of the following criteria?

1) Causes an ice age

2) Causes mass extinction

3) Causes nanocrystals in the ice, only known to form in the presence of extreme heat.

Based on what we think we know of human history, we assume humans lived in caves 50,000 years ago.

Then again, the further back we look in known history, the more advanced so called "ancient" technologies were. What then, does that say of our knowledge or, rather, ignorance of what might have been happening here on Earth 50,000 years ago?

Our current cultural beliefs and prejudices support as much conjecture as truth.

Try this little thought experiment. Remove the single most fundamental assumption we make about pre-history: Ancient humans were primitive.

Remove that prejudice two assumptions, and consider what equally probable "theory" emerges in their absence. It is one which, given identical evidence, interpreted through a radically different viewpoint, seems at least equally as probable. If we don't learn from history, we'll be doomed to repeat it.

◇

And as for the nanocrystals in the ice?

To date, we have found nano-crystals such as those in only two places on Earth: 1) meteor impact craters; and 2) areas where nuclear devices have been detonated.

Reincarnation of Civilization

*M*any *of the* oldest world religions hold that there has been three incarnations of civilization. (Ours is the third). The Great Flood offers possible evidence for a transition between the second and third incarnations. But three?

Is it even plausible?

It's hard to say. But what I do believe is that our civilization, even our science has a very myopic view of history.

When we think about Ancient Civilizations, we talk about the Greeks, the Sumerians, the Chinese, perhaps even the Maya. These are all ancient Empires that rose, thrived, declined and died within the past 8,000 years or so—meaning they are all examples of cultures in our current incarnation of civilization.

Viewed this way, all of the world empires, cultures, and ways of life that fill our history books are all parts of one civilization—ours.

It the ultimate exercise in ethnocentrism to believe that our civilization of the past 5,000 years is the be-all end-all of civilization on Earth.

There are inexplicable similarities between many known cultures which likely never had contact with one another— similarities modern anthropologists are at a loss to explain. Take for example the pyramids of Africa and South America. Not only is their construction similar, their astronomical alignments are identical.

Many world religions believe in human re-incarnation after death. (Western tradition scoffs at this.) Likewise, many mythologies hold that civilization has also been reincarnated three times. Western tradition scoffs at this as well.

Seems this quick dismissal by western men of science exemplifies our quick-to-dismiss mentality much more than it disproves the possibility of civilized-reincarnation.

Most of us (if we really do have past lives) don't remember them. So, if there's any credibility to the notion of civilized-reincarnation, it might stand to reason that each successive reincarnation might have no knowledge of its past life and death cycle.

Many religions teach that the universe is cyclical. Why should civilization be any different?

It the ultimate exercise in ethnocentrism to believe that our civilization of the past 5,000 years is the be-all end-all of civilization on Earth.

Once again, it comes back to the dismissive Western ideology that man is separate and unequal from nature.

Science will likely never accept the possibility of reincarnation because science is handicapped by believing only what can be proven.

◇

Yet there may be circumstantial evidence for the reincarnation of civilization, such as the paradox of the pyramids.

One explanation for their similarity is that both the Maya and the Egyptians had similar knowledge, passed down from a forgotten incarnation of civilization.

Or, perhaps that previous incarnation of civilization built both sets of pyramids themselves, perhaps before plate tectonics separated Egypt and Africa.

Perhaps the end of the last incarnation of civilization was somehow linked to some global event powerful enough to cause continental drift at an extremely accelerated rate.

The possibilities for conjecture abound. Most are probably best left to the realm of Science Fiction. And I'm not advocating any of these ideas as fact.

I am advocating the evolution of thought necessary to consider them. Because 100 years ago, going to the moon was
science fiction.

So was the atom bomb.

So was breaking the sound barrier.

So is breaking the light barrier.

So is time travel.

You don't have to 'go somewhere' to get beyond civilization.
You have to make your living a different way.

– Daniel Quinn

On and on you will hike
and I know you'll hike far
and face up to your problems˙
whatever they are.

You'll get mixed up, of course,
as you already know.

So be sure when you step,
step with care and great tact
and remember that Life's
a Great Balancing Act.

Oh, the places you'll go.

– Dr. Seuss

Part V

Oh The Places ~~You'll~~ *we could* Go.

Nature Deficit Disorder

he lost world that emerges from the chrysalis of the rain-forest when one penetrates the interior truly is the prover-bial somewhere over the rainbow. It's a world that morphs Jules Vernes' Center of the Earth and Tolkien's *Middle Earth* into one. Horned spiders and nocturnal frogs with translucent bodies live there, alongside lizards who walk on water. Cures for tumors, asthma, malaria and depression can be found in the leaves of the most commonplace (by rainforest standards) variety of flora. There are venomous snakes immune to the toxins of poison frogs, and sap from certain leaves is a hundred times more deadly than cyanide to humans. Ancient Kapoks (giants among trees) stand astride Walking Palms, and together weave a canopy overhead that's inhabited by the regal Red Howlers along with five other species of monkeys.

> We have become so far removed as a civilization that we have forsaken Nature. Perhaps the most serious pandemic the modern world has ever seen is the "Green Plague," Nature Deficit Disorder.

But they're coming to get you, all of you, my dears. These verdant trenches of the jungle interior—home to a million billion other beings we've neither dreamed nor seen—are the front lines in the most horrific biological warfare humanity has ever waged. This is where oil companies don't fear to tread.

The pristine, untouched stillness of a world few humans will experience will likely not exist in precious few decades if the corporations continue having their way.

We have become so far removed as a civilization that we have forsaken Nature. Our cities team with chronic illness, depression, anxiety and perhaps the most serious pandemic the modern world has ever seen—the "Green Plague," Nature Deficit Disorder.

The frog does not drink up the pond in which he lives, so goes the Native American proverb. But we now do.

And all the while, as this is happening right under our noses, most people I've met, like amnesiacs, seem to be vaguely aware there's something they're forgetting. But they can't quite put their finger on what. We must draw a line in the oil sands. Much has been written about how it is not too late—how there's still time to change our fate. But we humans don't have all the time in the world. (Only the Earth does.)

So what can we do? I'm not a political activist—I simply don't have the stomach for it. And I don't really want to hunt whaling boats from rubber rafts, either.

We can't rely on international groups to do the dirty work. The Earth does not belong to anyone; but each of us according to our abilities must defend it.

I've heard that some other guy once said: *each according to his ability.* The phrase has been attributed to everyone from Louis Blanc, Henri de Saint Simon, Jesus in the New Testament, and Carl Marx. (Imagine being a fly on the wall at that poker game.) No one knows for sure who coined the phrase. Personally, I like to think it was the first aborigine to ever lay eyes on an invading Western army of Capitalists. Actually, what he said was, "Oh, shit. There goes the planet." But some things get lost in translation.

Today, we are witnessing humanity's relationship with nature approaching a critical threshold. If we blink, it may be gone.

Some things are being done. The United Nations' program to reduce emissions from deforestation (UN-REDD) is meeting with some promising success. The international community such as the United Nations, the World Wildlife Fund and others are doing what they can. But we can't rely on international groups to do all the dirty work.

The question is, what can you and I do?

Each according to his ability.

The Earth does not belong to anyone; but everyone must do their part to defend it from the cannibals. If the series of global crises we face are to "dissolve into collective solutions," as the documentary The 11th Hour so poetically puts it, those solutions must emerge not from global powers, but from the efforts and intentions of people like you and me. To each according to his ability.

Last year, I met a native Kichwa guide building an eco-lodge in the South of Equador. He and I shared a meeting of the minds. He told me the eco-tourism dollars his lodge brings in are returned to the local community, to protect the people and the forest.

The most important butterfly effect of all will be the metamorphosis of our world view, and the best way of achieving that is one person at a time.

We need more initiatives like this on the individual level.

Because the truth is, time is running out.

Global Warning

During the Cold War, a magazine called the *Bulletin of the Atomic Scientists* published at the University of Chicago developed an idea they called the Doomsday Clock. On the cover of the first issue in 1947, the clock's hands were set at seven minutes to midnight.

The symbolism was that nuclear genie we had unleashed had brought humanity desperately close to the destruction of civilization.

In today's world, the threat of nuclear war takes a back-seat to our current parabolic trajectory of collapse. Beginning a nuclear war involves some dictator, zealot or ideologue actually pushing the button. Actually choosing to destroy the whole world.

It could happen.

But in today's world of convergent global catastrophes, it's *not acting* that's causing the minute hand to tick ever closer towards midnight.

◇

We have a doomsday clock for nuclear war; we even have a ticking clock for our national debt. Today we need a doomsday clock to measure Co_2 emissions.

According to the International Energy Agency, as of November 2011, we were at five years to midnight. By 2016, we'll be trapped in a scenario of "perilous climate change." The idea is that by measuring the total global Co_2 concentration in the atmosphere, we can tell when we will reach the tipping point.

Theoretically, when the Co_2

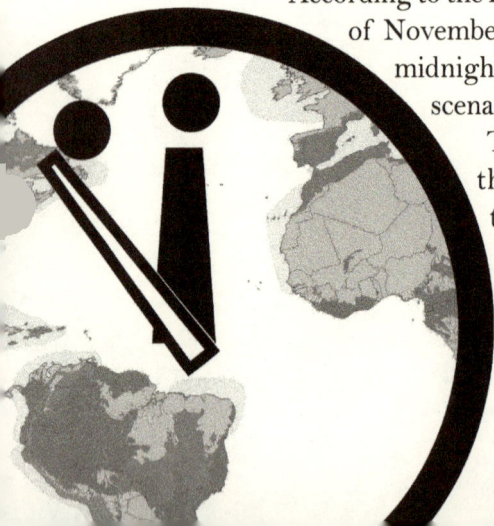

concentration in the atmosphere reaches 450 parts per million—that's the magic number which starts a chain reaction—global warming will spiral out of control.

We need a CO_2 parts-per-million clock.
That's today's version of doomsday.

Today's current level of CO_2 is 390 ppm. 450 ppm is going to happen by 2016, according to the IEA. The CO_2 emitted over the next 5 years is projected to be roughly 40% of the total emitted since 1900.

So we need a CO_2 parts-per-million clock.

That's today's version of doomsday.

iTrek

---

*W*riters *(but more* so readers) have an important part to play in any change we can hope to see in the world. The written word (be it online in blog or, my personal preference, in a book) remains the most effective means to spread ideas. No other form of media is so equipped to express and deliver the kind of thoughtful, comprehensive ideas that can be the only effective weapon against the weapon of mass destruction wielded by politician and corporations: *the Soundbite.*

Literature—the written word—can deliver a message not only of hope, but help each of us build a brave new world in which hope does not seem a foolishly childish illusion.

Revolutions have been started by words.

Thomas Paine's "Common Sense" was so influential that John Adams said, "Without the pen of the author of 'Common Sense,' the sword of Washington would have been raised in vain."

But it was not Paine who started the American Revolution. It was his readers. They heard a call to action.

Likewise, readers of *The Communist Manifesto* by Karl Marx created a whole new form of government. Good ideas as well as bad spread like a plague through books of all genres.

It has been said that if we can imagine it, we can build it.

Every employee of Apple must be a die-hard Trekky. Nearly everything Apple invents comes right out of Star Trek.

I believe that in a very tangible way, the world we have today was built not by science, but by science fiction.

Science fiction was a genre that only came into its own about 150 years ago. Science fiction began with authors like Jules Verne and H.G. Wells, who are considered the "Fathers of Science Fiction," who were so inspired by the new mechanical, scientific age, that they started imagining all sorts of ideas, including space travel, airplanes, life under water, and time travel. They brought these ideas to life in fictional futures they imagined.

A century and a half later, many of these far-fetched science fiction stories are happening in the real world .... every day in airports around the world, military submarines, and NASA.

Most of today's most cutting edge science was first imagined by writers, not by scientists.

And in a very real way, the techno-geeky world of pads and pods and tablets, oh my, is a direct result of the hugely influential TV series Star Trek.

Every employee of Apple must be a die-hard Trekky. Nearly everything Apple invents comes right out of Star Trek.

Look for the original Apple computer monitors and floppy disk drives in the original series which aired in the 1960s.

Desktop computers in the 1960s? Yep, they were even in the home of millions of Americans. By way of TV.

Then there's the iPad. In Star Trek, a handheld tablet-style devise is known as a *P.A.D.D.* (Personal Access Display Device).

And the inventions transcend Apple labs.

Take cell phones. In the year 2000, I had one called the "Star Tac," which flipped up the same way as William Shatner's did forty years ago. The only thing missing was the trademark *deedle-dilldle-deep* sound effect.

How about a USB drive? These have today all but completely erased floppy disks and the 3.5" diskette, just as they were replaced in the next generation of Star Trek with what were called *Isolinear Chips.*

I'm sure the Trekkies at Apple could offer up a whole laundry list of modern technology that came right out of Star Trek or other works of Science Fiction.

The point is, much of the world we have today was dreamed

up in the minds of science fiction writers. The point is, anything we dream we can build.

If we dream of a world of unlimited renewable energy, time travel, light-speed vehicles, an abundant food supply, no possessions, a brotherhood of man, living life in peace, then we can build it.

The Power of One

"Books can teach, illuminate, and even inspire. But they can do so only to the extent that humans are determined to use them to those ends." —**Edward R. Murrow**

urrow, an iconic American journalist of the 1950 and 60s, was speaking about television at the time, but the same holds true for every form of mass media.

Some of the most important written words that see the light of today's world must focus on raising awareness and consciousness in all of us as individuals and as a species. Our books must further environmental protection and activism, and inspire and encourage the best parts of human nature to shine forth.

The subjects and topics of the most important literary achievements in today's age and their authors must not hide sheepishly under the rug. They must be bold, decisive and brave, when it comes to identifying and decrying an immediate call to action to halt the worst atrocities any species has ever committed in the history of Earth against ourselves and our planet.

Literature that does this effectively, if there is any, will be regarded as important works by any future generations, if there are any. They will be on par with Thomas Pain's *Common Sense*, and Marx's *Manifesto* as far as books (other than religious texts) that change the world are concerned.

The means by which literature must accomplish these ends is by changing individual lives and worldviews.

Only by the widespread dissemination of actionable ideas and action by enough individuals can the world change. Only by changing enough individuals' minds can the world itself can be changed.

Why do I place such onus on individuals? Because any single

group that becomes singularly large enough to effectively fight the hierarchy of the establishment, must have, in its requisite size, itself already been transformed into a hierarchy. That's why it's up to individuals, individually, to make a difference. We must allow the solidarity of our thoughts and action unite us. A changing worldview will be exponentially more effective than any committees, groups or confederations we can possibly form.

◇

In the planned next volume of this series currently being researched, I will endeavor to uncover the best, most influential and creative ideas currently in practice by pioneers who are beginning the transition into a new world and laying the foundation for the rest of us.

But don't let me (or them) stop you from doing your own research and making your own changes right now!

What can you do?

"Television records in black and white and in color, evidence of decadence, escapism, and insulation from the realities of the world in which we live. We are currently wealthy, fat, comfortable, and complacent. We have a built in allergy to unpleasant or disturbing information; our mass media reflect this.

"We must get up off our fat surpluses and recognize that media, in the main, is being use to distract, delude, amuse, and insulate us. Media can teach, it can illuminate; yes, and it can even inspire. But it can do so only to the extent that humans are determined to use it to those ends."
—Edward R. Murrow

Never doubt that a small group of thoughtful, committed citizens can change the world. Indeed, it is the only thing that ever has.
—Margaret Mead

Till Transition Do We Part

*O*ur *culture is* obsessed with viewing all transitions as
death warrants.

Death, the ultimate transition from this life to ... whatever's next, is regarded as something to be dreaded, worried
about, fretted over, cheated.

We are pathologically frightened of change. It keeps us going
to work at jobs we hate, relationships that are abusive, or living
lives we don't enjoy.

We view global warming as the potential death knell of civilization. Well, it might very well be. But we can choose to look
at it from a vastly different perspective.

Global warming, which may trigger the collapse our own current way of life, is not the death of anything but a transition
into a brave new world, perhaps into the next incarnation of
civilization which will know nothing of this one.

*There's still time to ensure that global warming isn't the death
of civilization as we know it, but merely a transition
away from a self-destructive way of life.*

Realists today admit global warming exists.

Optimists believe there's something we can do about it.

Pessimists believe there's nothing we can do about it and it's
going to be anarchy.

I think it's about time all of us start believing all of the above.
I believe the Earth likely has already reached the tipping point
where the global warming process can not be reversed. We may
not have reached the holy grail of 450 ppm Co_2, but we're beyond
the point of turning back now.

I believe it's time we start accepting there's nothing we can do to prevent our fate. The sooner we accept that, the sooner we can begin to get about the work of figuring out what we're going to do next. If we can come up with workable alternatives, there's still time to ensure that global warming isn't the death of civilization as we know it, but merely a transition away from a self-destructive way of life, a way of life we may be much happier living without ... if we can learn now.

Either way, a transition is coming. It offers a gateway into a brave new world. The world that lies through that wormhole will be whatever we make of it.

How To Build An Ark

*D*on't *limit yourself* to what you're told you can see with your own eyes. There is so much more that we can perceive.

They are your eyes. Use them to see what you wish.

Question what you're told.

Take control of your own health.

Take control of your own way of life.

Add life to your years.

Question reality.

Cut corporate control out of your life.

Buy only from individuals or local merchants.

◇

How to navigate your ark:

• We must live locally. Eat locally, travel only as far as a bicycle can take you (no oil, no cars).

• Grow our own food; source locally grown items; or create and support Community Supported Agricultural movements. Local co-ops are good, too.

• Use only energy locally generated renewably.

• Hang your clothes out to dry in the sun.

• Live close to a fresh water source.

• Lessen your dependence on money.

• Make sure your career supports not only your family but your neighbors.

When oil prices triple, it won't prove economical to drive to a job that pays the same as it always had. In other words, it won't make economic sense to work in an office far, far away. And if you're still addicted to money then to provide for your basic needs, you might be in trouble.

I'm not advocating donating your money to charity or living in squalor. Simply work to find ways to provide for your most fundamental necessities (water, food, etc.) that doesn't involve buying them.

And perhaps most importantly of all, create a strong sense of community where you live. This may involve an exodus from the cities and suburbs into small towns and communities.

Cities are more dependent on infrastructure than towns and rural areas. We're seeing a rise in urban agriculture, but in its current state, the speed it's gaining momentum won't be sufficient.

I believe cities will be traps whenever grocery stores are unable to take daily shipments of staples.

We all must rely on each other, not a hierarchy of laws, economics, corporate interests, oil and politicians for our day-to-day survival.

No this isn't a Libertarian philosophy. I don't believe we all should become self-sufficient survivalists.

I believe that only with each other's help can we all survive ... and return to a quality of life we haven't known in centuries.

We all must, once again, re-learn how to rely on real people. Sorry, facebook people and twitter people are not real people. You may think of them as your best friends, but if you don't see them every day or sit in the same room with them every day or live within walking or biking distance, you're not relying on them for your day-to-day survival, and you won't be able to.

We must learn how to rely on our local communities—real people who we see everyday.

How To Navigate An Ark

"Whether or not it is clear to you,
no doubt the universe is unfolding as it should."
—Max Ehrmann, Desiderata

One of the hopes that has been manifest in People since the dawn of civilization itself was living in a perfect world, achieving utopia. Among many reasons, it was that hope which drove us out of the grasslands and jungles.

"Things are nice here," I'm sure we thought. "But we can make them better." That's when we started to become farmers, in order to control our food supply.

The solution to one problem always leads to another problem to solve. We layer solution upon problem upon problem upon solution.

That's where we balked. Our desire to improve is not truly our downfall; but intrinsic in that desire is a grasping mind of ill-content.

Our idea was sound: we can grow our own grain. But the underlying, unspoken ideology of a culture who believes it must control its own food supply is: the Universe is not unfolding as it should.

With plentiful food, we banded together in larger towns and cities. That idea was sound enough, too: we should build community. But the mistake there was that because a small community is good, a large community is better.

We soon encountered problems in large cities, and when someone proclaimed, "I can solve this problem!" and did, he was elected sovereign.

That idea was also sound: someone should lead us. But intrinsic therein is the idea that without leadership is anarchy. And that's true, too, but only in large groups.

We should have seen at this point that the solution to one problem always leads to another problem to solve. But we didn't. And we layered solution upon problem upon problem upon solution. Civilization is the story of endlessly inventive solutions to man-made problems.

And so it went through thousands of years of sovereigns and slaves. Always grasping, but never quite attaining. Cultures and Empires rose and fell, and always we began again.

Oppression led to revolution.

Revolution: a sound enough idea. If governments aren't working, overthrow it. But revolution is not exempt from our problem/solution paradigm.

What we never realize is whenever David defeats Goliath, David becomes Goliath.

And so we grasped some more.

While the plebeians dreamed of a lives of leisure, the plutocracy dreamed of more wealth.

The dream of civilization achieving utopia was quietly buried among the rubble of thousands of years of toil and servitude and empires rising and falling.

Then it happened that there were so many of us that we began consuming the world. Forests started disappearing as we used them for timber, or burned them for heat.

Then there were more of us still that now we outgrew the trees.

Then, a spark.

A machine.

A machine to work better, faster, quicker, more efficiently than all of us combined.

The Industrial Revolution was a quantum leap in the evolution of civilization, one which led to the resurgence of our utopian dream. We saw how the incredible capacity of these wonderful machines had doubled, tripled, quadrupled mankind's productivity.

And laborers believed that since infinitely more was being accomplished in an hour, a much shorter work-day would be soon at hand.

A reasonable thought to have. And it would have, should have, could have been possible.

But for the slave drivers, the captains of industry, enough is never enough.

While the plebeians dreamed of a lives of leisure, the plutocracy dreamed of more wealth.

The Industrial Age was being fueled with oil.

If we consumed today only as much oil as we used at the turn of the 20th century, fossil fuels could probably have powered the world for 10,000 years.

It was a brilliant idea, really, to tap into Earth's resources to provide energy, but the possibility that those reserves could ever run dry was never conceived of.

Of course, if we still consumed today only as much oil as we used at the turn of the 20th century, fossil fuels could probably have powered the world for 10,000 years. But today, we no longer live within our means. But our usage has increased 1,000 in 100 years. And so the dream of utopia was consumed by the flames of greed. But it didn't take 10,000 years for it to be-reborn again. This time, it only took 100.

The age of computers dawned and our productivity quadrupled yet again, and the phoenix of hope rose from the ashes.

We could all be working four-hour days and society would still thrive. We'd all have family time, vacation time, time to spend our hard-earned money, embrace the possibility of world travel and so on and a life of leisure.

In socialist-leaning Europe today, for the middle-class, some of this has manifested. Government regulations call for a minimum of five weeks of vacation for every employee (including new hires from day one.)

That's nothing to sneeze at. It's the closest that the largest number of humans have ever come to realizing true lives of leisure in the history of our civilization.

But still that is luxury reserved for the middle class, wedged between the ultra-rich and the incomprehensibly poor.

Social inequality remains as insurmountable a gulf as ever.

But, still, we are closer than ever today to the utopian society that hundred of thousands of generations of humans have dreamed of.

Closer than ever. And yet it could all slip away. There are a lot of roadblocks.

But this is no time to stop dreaming. The proof of the power of imagination is all around us. (I will not use what I believe has become a pejorative and corrupted phrase: the power of intention. In concept, the theory of "intention" is sound.)

We could have a world filled with roads, railroads, cities, skyscrapers, airplanes, satellites, rockets to the moon. All that and so much more. We just have to imagine a way to have it without expending non-renewable resources. I have no doubt such a world can exist.

Imagine what else we can imagine.

Perhaps it's Tesla's theory of free, wireless, renewable electricity that paves the way. Perhaps it's when we finally learn to live within our means. Perhaps it's some new idea, some new technology not even conceived of yet.

Most likely it is a convergence of all of the above.

None of what we have today could ever have existed in the first place, had it not been imagined by visionaries who dared to dream.

We have manifested a wondrous world of modern marvels. Just look all around you. It's truly incredible what we've built, how far we've come, in just the past 100 years alone. We are magicians of the first order. There is seemingly no limit to what we can manifest with the power of our thoughts alone.

We are a creative species. We are endlessly inventive. For good or for ill, we alone living in the tree of life have coalesced into an advanced, technological civilization.

We have wind, earth elements, fire and air, and nothing more. The trick lies in combining them in ways each previous generation had never before considered.

We started from nothing more than mud and dirt and elements of Earth, stones and green-leafy vegetables. That's all we've ever had and all we ever will have—Earth and her resources.

We can dream of resources that abound on the moon and stars, but there are no spaceships ready-made, waiting for us there, nor solar panels to be found halfway to the sun.

No technology on Earth exists that we ourselves have not imagined first and then created out of simple elements combined in endlessly complex and inventive ways.

We have wind, earth elements, fire and air and nothing more. The trick lies in combining them in ways each previous generation had never before considered.

One day, we woke up in a world capable of producing magical devises that fly, transport, create, destroy, ruin and rebuild, fabricate and produce, digitize and swipe, beep and blast, make horrendous cacophonies and musical notes that stir us to the very the depths of our souls.

Imagine what else we can imagine.

Imagine the figments of imagination we can manifest.

The fault lies not in our failing to imagine a perfect world, but in our imagining an imperfect one.

Oh, the world we could imagine. Filled with things we can't even fathom.

Suggested Continued Reading

I do not endorse these authors as experts, as I despise any self-proclaimed experts. Rather, these are must-reads for inquiring minds who endeavor to think outside their own collective thoughts.

Books
(alpha by author)

Boyle, T.C.
Drop City

Brodie, Richard
Virus of the Mind

Chilton, Joseph Pierce
The Crack in the Cosmic Egg
Magical Child

Doidge, Norman, MD
The Brain that Changes Itself

Gilbert, Daniel
Stumbling on Happiness

Greene, Brian
The Eloquent Universe

Hartmann, Thom
The Prophet's Way
The Last Hours of Ancient Sunlight*

Gosswami, Amit
The Self-Aware Universe

Greene, Brian
The Hidden Reality:
Parallel Universes and the
Deep Laws of the Cosmos

Kreisberg, Glenn
Lost Knowledge of the
Ancients

Laney, Marti Olsen
The Introvert Advantage

Millman, Dan
Way of the Peaceful
Warrior

McTaggart, Lynn
The Intention Experiment

Moalem, Sharon, Dr.
Survival of the Sickest

Quinn, Daniel
*Ishmael**
Beyond Civilization

Ryan, Christopher
*Sex at Dawn**

Sheldrake, Rupert
Morphic Resonance:

Wolfe, David
*The SunFood Diet Success System**

Wolff, Robert
Original Wisdom

Zinn, Howard
*A People's History of the United States***

Other media
Wikimedia***

Documentaries
GasLand
In Defense of Food
The 11th Hour
Collapse*

* Life-Changing
**Eye-opening
***The Akashik Records of the 21st Century

About the Author

In addition to being a writer, Tom is a serial entrepreneur, the founder of ttDesigns, a web design company, and Scenes of Time: Nature and Wildlife Photography.

He has also worked as a Journalist and served in the Peace Corpse in Africa, where he taught English as a Second Language.

Tom is the author of three books. His non fiction works are *A People's History of Capitalism* and *The Evolution of Thought. Time Without End* is his first novel.

Tom lives in Kansas City, MO.

About the Publisher

Green Effect Media is an Indie Publisher founded in Chicago in 2008, currently based in Kansas City, MO. It publishes works by independent authors.

Green Ef fect Media

For publishing querries, e-mail publisher@greeneffectmedia.com.

Also by Tom Tortorich

Time Without End

From one of today's most imaginative authors comes the mind-bending series *Time Without End* perhaps best described as...

Fringe meets *The Celestine Prophecy*...

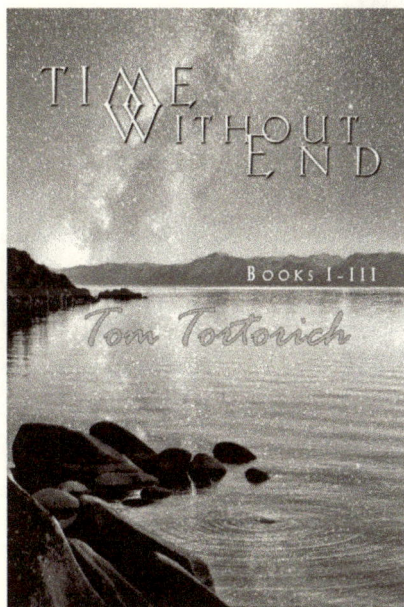

Erik and Rachel come from completely different worlds—parallel Earths, actually. But they have one thing in common: they have both taken evolution's next step. They are the first humans since the dawn of history able to pull themselves out of time and experience other realms of existence. Is this a power all of humanity will develop in time?

Readers accompany Erik and Rachel on a vision quest across parallel universes as they realize there are forces at work attempting to prevent human evolution. But why? And how?

A quest to the dawn of human history...
and civilization's end ...

Their quest reveals the truth about the beginnings of humanity itself, the ancient "Maygyptian" Empire, before the Ancient Maya and Egyptian civilizations were separated into parallel universes by the same intelligence now attempting to halt human evolution.

Also by Tom Tortorich

A People's History of Capitalism

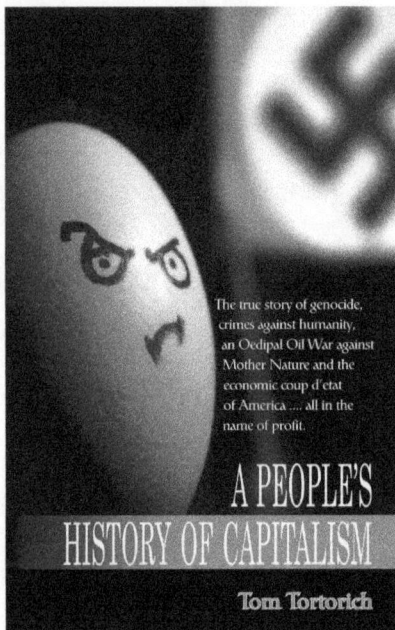

The true story of genocide, crimes against humanity, an Oedipal Oil War against Mother Nature and the economic coup d'etat of America .... all in the name of profit.

A PEOPLE'S
HISTORY OF CAPITALISM

Tom Tortorich

This left-wing view of Capitalism explores how the history of the past 500 years of Western Civilization has been driven by a singular obsession: the accumulation of ever-more wealth.

Reminiscent of Howard Zinn's A People History of the United States, this leftist economic perspective poses some powerful questions.